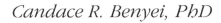

Candace R. Benyei, PhD

D0743868

Understanding Clergy Misconduct in Religious Systems
Scapegoating, Family Secrets, and the Abuse of Power

Pre-publication
REVIEWS,
COMMENTARIES,
EVALUATIONS . . .

"**I**n this masterful treatise, Candace Benyei courageously examines one of the religious community's better-kept secrets. With the zeal of a prophet, she reflects on the abuse of power and the perversion of trust in faith communities. This book is bound to create much controversy and disturb the complacent. Once having diagnosed the malady, Benyei leaves us with thoughtful and creative directions for healing. A must-read for therapists, clergy, and church leaders."

Elliot J. Rosen, EdD
Director,
Family Institute of Westchester,
Mt. Vernon, NY

"**B**enyei's book is clearly an important, thoughtful contribution to the topic in a timely context of unfortunately waning interest. This work is a welcome addition to a new generation of research that situates the misconduct of trusted leaders among traditions of faith in the essential context of religious institutions and belief systems. In her profound regard for faith traditions and people, Benyei's responsibly annotated understanding of this global failure is her comprehensive perspective in detailing the isolates of misconduct and resurrecting critical anchors of hope."

Fr. Roman Paur, OSB, PhD
Executive Director,
Interfaith Sexual Trauma Institute,
Collegeville, MN

More pre-publication
REVIEWS, COMMENTARIES, EVALUATIONS . . .

"Dr. Benyei has written a most interesting and informative book about clergy sexual misconduct. As noted in the foreword, this book is a contribution to the second generation of study and resources on this difficult topic. Dr. Benyei's perspective expands the conceptualization of clergy sexual misconduct beyond that of a freestanding, individually driven occurrence (the approach taken in most texts on the subject) to an occurrence within a community that is affected by a wide range of community issues and dynamics. This book is at once an unflinching look at a topic that is controversial and painful and simultaneously an empathic discussion of many factors that come into play when clergy misconduct occurs. Highly recommended reading for members of both the clergy and the laity."

Christine A. Courtois, PhD
*Independent Psychologist
and Clinical Director,
The CENTER: Posttraumatic
Disorders Program,
The Psychiatric Institute
of Washington,
Washington, DC*

"While writing this blurb, I received a call from across the continent, from a rabbi seeking help in handling a problem of sexual inappropriateness between a staff member and a prominent layperson in his congregation. The galleys of Dr. Benyei's book lay helplessly in front of me. Had the book been out, I would have sent him a copy immediately. I would have referred him especially to the chapters dealing with clergy sexual misconduct, secrets, and reowning responsibility. Dr. Benyei's book is a much-needed resource. It should be on the desk of those who serve in congregations and in the heads of those of us whose job it is to assist both clergy and congregations in dealing with the dynamic issues that can so upset congregational life. This book can go a long way toward making congregations and their clergy safer for each other."

Jack H. Bloom, PhD
*Director of Professional Review,
The Central Conference
of American Rabbis,
The Psychotherapy Center,
Fairfield, CT*

The Haworth Pastoral Press
An Imprint of The Haworth Press, Inc.

Understanding Clergy Misconduct in Religious Systems

Scapegoating, Family Secrets, and the Abuse of Power

THE HAWORTH PASTORAL PRESS
Religion and Mental Health
Harold G. Koenig, MD
Senior Editor

New, Recent, and Forthcoming Titles:

Understanding Clergy Misconduct in Religious Systems
Scapegoating, Family Secrets, and the Abuse of Power

Candace R. Benyei, PhD

The Haworth Pastoral Press
An Imprint of The Haworth Press, Inc.
New York • London

Published by

The Haworth Pastoral Press, an imprint of The Haworth Press, Inc., 10 Alice Street, Binghamton, NY 13904-1580

Cover design by Marylouise E. Doyle.

Library of Congress Cataloging-in-Publication Data

Benyei, Candace Reed.
    Understanding clergy misconduct in religious systems : scapegoating, family secrets, and the abuse of power / Candace R. Benyei.
        p.   cm.
    Includes bibliographical references and index.
    ISBN 0-7890-0452-6 (alk. paper).
    1. Sexual misconduct by clergy. I. Title.
BV4392.5.B45   1998
262'.1—dc21   97-37001
                                                                                                                      CIP

To all those who have had the courage to pursue justice,
because without justice, there is no healing.

ABOUT THE AUTHOR

Candace R. Benyei, MPS, PhD, a graduate of the New York Theological Seminary, is a spiritual director, research scientist, and teaching psychotherapist. Dr. Benyei is a nationally accredited supervisor and clinical member of the American Association of Marriage and Family Therapists and a regular member of the Society of Professionals in Dispute Resolution. She is Director of the Institute for Human Resources, maintains a private practice of congregational conflict resolution, and is an adjunct professor in Family Therapy at Fairfield University. She lives with her husband and children on a farm in Redding, Connecticut.

CONTENTS

Foreword

Since the mid-1980s in the United States and Canada, a new and distinct professional field has developed, that of preventing and responding to clergy abuses of power. It was at this time that significant numbers of victims/survivors of clergy sexual abuse first found their voices and their courage. Somehow, by the grace of God, church and synagogue began to hear those voices. The legal system helped this along considerably, but there also was a receptivity on the part of religious systems that had not been there before. As faith communities responded, progress has had a one-step-forward, two-steps-back quality to it. However, profound changes have occurred, and there is no returning to the days of secrecy, cover-ups, and denial.

When we began our research as a group of colleagues in 1989, we had a lot of questions. We found some answers to those questions, but for each answer, there emerged at least ten more questions. This continues today, and we discover that the complexity of this field is immense.

Now we are moving into the "second generation" of our development. This book represents a contribution to that second generation. Borrowing freely from insights into human behavior gleaned from many disciplines, this work places those insights within a theological context. Religious systems have much in common with other institutions, but they are also unique.

Faith communities are places where we bring our longings for meaning, intimacy, and deep connection with the Divine. People can be particularly vulnerable in faith communities. Many of our hopes, dreams, and yearnings are unspoken. The relationship between clergy and laity is often called upon to bear more than it is capable of bearing. This strain puts clergy at risk to offend, especially when they do not understand the power that is inherent in their role.

Yet, there are many other ways in which clergy are relatively powerless. The same dynamics that confer power—transference, projection, object relations, embodiment of the Divine, access to people in vulnerable moments—can have unintended, negative outcomes for clergy. While false accusations of sexual misconduct that are not quickly determined to be frivolous still continue to be rare, clergy seem to be increasingly under siege in a wide variety of ways and too quickly targeted as "the problem to be removed" in troubled congregations. This is certainly mirrored in the wider culture; all leaders seem to have lost a huge measure of trust and respect.

We must ask ourselves, however, if we have unwittingly contributed to this trend. We must view clergy power abuse as operating in interlocking systems within the context of the culture and the times. The job of prevention is only half accomplished if we work with just the clergy. Congregations also must understand the dynamics and learn to take more responsibility for their own spiritual growth. This book is not only for clergy or religious leaders but for their congregations as well.

The task that lies ahead is formidable, but not impossible. Breaking new ground is at once frightening and exhilarating. Ultimately, we are about the reclaiming of power and responsibility of laity who would truly share ministry with those who are ordained.

Nancy Myer Hopkins, MS
Member, Executive Board of the Interfaith
Sexual Trauma Institute;
Editor, *Restoring the Soul of a Church*

Preface

It has been said that "fools walk in where angels fear to tread." Most of us do not want to look at our families of faith with an unveiled face, and I am aware that some may find the material in these pages to be controversial or even offensive. However, it is my conviction that in a time when persons are discovering spiritual experience outside of traditional families of faith, if our current religious institutions are to survive, congregants, judicatory administrators, denominational executives, seminary students, and clergy, as well as the persons who counsel them, need to squarely face the facts of scapegoating, family secrets, and clergy misconduct that manifest in our midst. Moreover, we need to understand how and why these dynamics occur so that we can stop being reactors and take remedial action or even assume a proactive position.

The public outrage against clergy sexual misconduct is a relatively recent phenomenon, although as we now know, the behavior is long-standing because offending clergy have been protected by their institutional peers. While public outcry has helped to raise consciousness and, along with the courts, begun the process of prevention, it has also severely damaged the self-esteem and public image of hard-working and dedicated clergy professionals at large—persons who have already been under siege in an increasingly secularized and materially oriented world. As members of religious institutions, we need to be proactive with respect to the selection as well as the nurturance of our spiritual leaders.

However, clergy misconduct is not the sole sin. In most instances, our congregations are equally responsible, as in many ways, they also have participated in the keeping of the secret. In order to protect cherished illusions of the clergyperson as parent/protector/god, as well as the fantasy of the perfect family, congregants have scapegoated the truth-tellers and deeply damaged their families of faith. Secret-keeping has proved more abusive, in the long run, than the original incident. We also need to be proactive with respect to ordering our "family" affairs and the health and "wellness" of our faith communities.

On the walls of my office, amongst the paraphernalia of a collector of objects, hang two items in particular. One is an etching of the calling of Isaiah, illustrating the hot coal being held to his lips. As spiritual leaders, we are entrusted with a sacred duty and required to speak the truth. Instead, we have become a nation of people with unclean lips. We need to discover the courage to change that.

The other item is a work of calligraphy given to me by one of my clients. It is a saying by Bernie Siegel, a physician well known for his work with exceptional cancer patients, patients committed to the concept of self-healing rather than opting for a "magic bullet" from the medical environment. The letters spell out the following message:

> Choose life and teach
> those around you to live
> and become immortal
> in the only way possible—
> through love.

It is time for all the People of God to address the present cancer in our religious institutions, to choose life, and to model what we preach, laity and professionals alike. It is time for us to teach love to ourselves and to one another. I hope in these pages I have loved enough to help us do that.

Candace Reed Benyei

Acknowledgments

I wish to thank Nancy Hopkins and Buddy Hubbard for their helpful feedback with regard to the presentation of case material, and Sigrid Benyei and Marguerite Scinto for their invaluable support during the process of preparing this manuscript. I also wish to thank all the denominational staff persons who contributed up-to-date information with regard to the current treatment of matters germane to this writing, as well as to Rabbi Joe Davidson for his willingness to serve as a mentor and consultant who deepened my understanding of the Jewish faith and way of life.

Again I saw all the oppressions that are practiced under the sun. And behold the tears of the oppressed, and they had no one to comfort them. On the side of the oppressors there was power, and there was no one to comfort them.

Ecc. 4:1

Chapter 1

The Congregation As a Family System

Human beings are community animals. In the Beginning . . . or so it goes, God created not one, but two humans in relationship. Ever since Eden we have lived in interconnecting groups, beginning with our families and then extending to social, professional, and religious organizations, the workplace, the greater community in which we live, and finally states and nations. Each of these groups, or *systems*, has dynamics that transcend the action of individuals. Imagine a mobile or kinetic sculpture with varied forms suspended by thin strands from armatures of several lengths. One notices that when a single, shiny element is touched the whole system is energized. The entire construction spins softly through the air with each component describing its own particular orbit. No one component is independent of the others but functions according to its position in the system. Furthermore, if the sculpture is taken apart and the components are rearranged, each element will be seen to move in a different way or to have a different behavior. So it becomes apparent that the behavior of the components also differs according to where they are placed in relation to others.

In like manner, the religious community is not a gathering of separate persons, but an interrelated system.[1] Similar to the laws of physics that determine the motion of the elements in the mobile, the "orbits" that the members of the congregation turn in are defined by a set of laws or rules. These are some combination of formal or written rules, informal rules or unwritten, and implicit or unconscious rules that might be called "family messages." Some of these rules help the congregation function well, and some of them hinder it. All the rules of a community are an evolutionary product of its history.

The behavior of persons in the community is also determined by where they are placed in relation to others in the congregational structure. This has to do with issues of power, as well as what well-known family therapist, Murray Bowen, called the *family projection system*. This is the phenomenon that occurs when community members, in the manner of a motion-picture projector, play on each other an image of a part of themselves that they have not acknowledged or are unaware of. They then relate to one another, not according to who each really is but according to their projective assumptions about the other, as if that person actually had become the imagined figure.

Finally, systems are molded by their history—the events that they experience as a unit. Traumatic as well as ecstatic occurrences become part of the shared memory of the community, and the community's reaction to these occurrences becomes a predictor of future behavior under similar circumstances.

THE ROLE OF RULES

The Evolution of Structure

From the study of group dynamics, we know that when any group of persons comes together for any purpose, even if all the participants have previously been totally unrelated, the group will immediately begin to form rules. Some persons in the group will have a greater need for formal structure than other, and will prefer to have a stated agenda for group meetings and recognized leadership. Other persons will be more comfortable being spontaneous, and will prefer shared, informal leadership. There will be a tension in the group between those who want to elect a leader and have stated goals and objectives and those who want a more flexible, even egalitarian, structure whose work meets the ever-changing needs of the membership and whose leaders arise as their gifts are needed. The emerging balance of power in the group, as well as environmental influences, usually determines the outcome.

Entrepreneurial efforts, or business start-ups, usually are quick to develop a formal structure because they come together with a stated purpose already in mind, such as the production of a product and the making of money. Even consumer cooperatives that perhaps have shared leadership have defined ways of doing business, particularly as operations become more complex and a certain consistency is required.

Informal social groups, persons that associate because they enjoy one another's company, are probably on the other end of the spectrum. These groups do not come together to produce a product, but rather to enjoy one another's presence. They may, from time to time produce something, such as a flower show or a musical production, but the product may change as the needs of the group change. These groups will tend to have an informal structure. Families are a subset of this kind of group.

Religious institutions are somewhere in between formal and informal structures. Early on in Judeo-Christian history, the Israelites, under the initial leadership of Moses, developed a complex body of sacred law beginning with the Ten Commandments. Their community was a *theocracy*, which means that it was seen to be governed by God through the agent of a priestly order. The Ten Commandments represented a *rule of life*—an ethical guide for being in a community. The emphasis was not on the production of a product, but rather on creating a way of living together that reflected the holy.

Later on in its history, in the eleventh century BCE, the Israelite people decided that in order to survive in a land continually overrun by competing interests,[2] they needed a king to direct their military forces. First, they selected the charismatic but mentally unstable Saul, then David who united the northern and southern tribes, and then David's son, Solomon, who had a taste for wealth and power. Solomon forced his subjects to spend time away from their farms building royal buildings and serving in the larger armies needed to obtain goods and services by conquering the neighboring peoples. This caused many of the farmers to go bankrupt, giving them little choice but to sell their land for sustenance and their children into slavery. Monarchy forever transformed the lifestyle of the Israelite people from an egalitarian community of landed peasant farmers to a class system split between wealthy bureaucrats and priests and impoverished, now often tenant farmers and slaves. The rules had changed.

Jesus of Nazareth, as did the Hebrew prophets before him, preached a return to egalitarian and ethical community. The Christian Church was founded on this precept. However, by the time the Gospel writers had finished their task around the year 100 CE, formal structure was well on its way, along with the corruption inherent in the competition for position and status. Christians have spent the last almost 2,000 years struggling with the same issues of power and hierarchy versus egalitarian, ethical community that their forbears did.

Different Strokes: Formal, Informal, and Implicit Rules

As we have just seen, rules seem to fall into one of three categories: formal rules, informal rules, and implicit rules. With regard to communities of faith, formal rules are those such as constitutions and by-laws, books of order, canon law, and any published policies of the institution. Just as in the case of the Israelite people, these rules evolve to meet the growing need of the institution for structure as a result of the diversity of its tasks and the way it wants to be present in the world. These rules are public—arrived at by consensus and subject to amendment, by consensus, through a specified process. Most of the ordinary people in the pews have little knowledge of, or interest in these rules, as they mostly have to do with the legal structure of the institution. They are the stud walls behind the plaster, so to speak, and are rarely changed unless some remodeling needs to be done or the institution is in want of an addition.

Informal rules are conscious but not written down. They may include an unpublished dress code, such as "no jeans in church," or be other silently agreed upon behaviors such as "no children at the early morning service," or "stand during the prayers." These are important rules because they have to do with the public face, the ordering of everyday behavior, and the comfort of the congregation. One might liken them to the wallpaper that one must be careful not to deface. Members usually take care not to break informal rules for fear of disapproval or rejection. These rules are more difficult to change since there is no formal structure through which to amend or even discuss them.

Unconscious, or implicit rules, are neither written down nor are they part of the congregation's conscious awareness, or at least they are not generally acknowledged. In fact, if consciously examined, implicit rules can seem irrational, unfair, or objectionable. However, they govern the members' most intimate communication patterns as well as their most important behaviors. These rules are imparted to the congregation from the historic families of its members, particularly its leadership, as well as from evolutionary events. An example of such a rule might be, "Don't rock the boat." That is, don't do or say anything that will upset anybody. Oftentimes people are used to behaving in this way, having learned it in their families of origin, so they do it in their religious communities also.

Other rules might be, "Leaders can make decisions on their own" and "Do as you are told." Depending upon the structure of the denomination, these might be at least informal rules. However in the Christian free church denominations, as well as most Jewish denominations, major decisions are usually made by committee or even congregational consensus. Persons who come from families where one parent clearly has authority over the other, or persons who are used to making unilateral decisions in business, tend to bring this rule into the congregation by behaving in this way. If these persons are leaders in the congregation for a period of time, it is easy for the congregation to adopt this principle unaware. This rule is frequently found in family-sized[3] congregations.

A fourth rule might be, "Keep the secret" or its corollary, "Don't ask questions." This rule is often brought into the faith community by persons whose families experienced something that they perceived as shameful. If something bad, shameful, or disadvantageous occurs in the congregation, persons with this rule in their background will attempt to suppress knowledge of the event, or at least suppress conversation about it. Keeping the secret is also a common way of maintaining a position of power, as it impedes direct action by dissatisfied persons or examination by the entire community. For example, groups interested in concealing financial mismanagement by a beloved pastor might stall an audit and put subtle pressure on aware but ethically conflicted persons to stay silent. Such behavior requires a lot of energy, and eventually more and more persons will participate in both the knowing and the secret keeping. This rule, somewhat like a virus, tends to be highly contagious, and, as we shall see later in more detail, also facilitates the perpetuation of abuse. In its mildest form, the secrecy rule ensures that committee minutes will be scanty and the history of a process will be difficult to determine.

In general, the role of rules, be they formal, informal, or implicit, is to order the system and guide its workings in set ways. These rules, once formed, tend to be continuous throughout the life of the system. Formal rules will be amended as needed, and to a lesser extent. so will informal rules. However, implicit rules, because they are most usually unwritten, unspoken, and out of conscious awareness, are very difficult to change. They are passed down through the generations of the system's history through repetition and modeling, similar to the way that young children learn to walk and to talk. In many ways they become part of the "hardware" of the organism—the "motherboard" of the internal, human computer. Shifts in implicit rules require that they first be brought into conscious awareness. Then they can be subjected to a process of discernment and discarded or altered.

POWER AND PROJECTION

The Struggle for Survival

Looking back again to the book of Genesis, it seems that from the Judeo-Christian perspective most of humankind's difficulties arose when we decided to rely on our own resources instead of the gifts of a provident God. We ate the apple offered in order to know good and evil and to become like gods, or so the serpent had promised us. The Hebrew words used in the text for "good" and "evil" indicate that the fruit of this tree did not have to do with the ability to make just decisions, however.[4] Instead we acquired the deftness to obtain excess pleasure, gain, and profit, or the reverse, pain, loss, and desperation. Instead of discovering life, which we already had, we discovered insecurity, and its corollary, the need for power.

Power is the ability to influence an outcome. Most human battles are over power, to the extent that as children most of our games point toward winning or losing or indeed, practicing for that struggle. Power is often about survival in a world where it seems that we need to look out for number one, a situation that is fostered in families that are not good at nurturing their children and instead hold fast to the implicit rule, "You have to do it by yourself." As a result, we are often taught to accumulate advantage to ourselves instead of striving to enable equal opportunity for the other. We believe that there is not enough to go around or even that there *should* not be enough to go around.

Most of us have at least a small desire for the affirmation from our peers that the status of position gives us. It makes us feel all right and worthwhile. We are more secure because we are less likely to be discarded. Status, therefore, is power. The privilege that frequently accompanies position is also attractive because it gives us more choices, more freedoms, and even greater economic resources than our neighbor. It softens the sense of helplessness that has become part of the human condition, since by our own hand we were forced out of Eden. It is a terrible double bind to be helpless   as we certainly are in the face of many diseases, environmental circumstances such as war, and uncontrollable natural forces such as tornadoes—and yet solely responsible for one's survival. In fact, such helplessness can lead to desperation. Cain was so desperate for status in the eyes of God that he killed his brother Abel, when it seemed that Abel's offering was more pleasing (Gen 4:3-9).

Advantage is a powerful determinant in relationships. We tend to limit our behavior based on our level in a hierarchy, sort of a pecking order as it were. We do not disobey the rules of the majority or cause displeasure to those that we perceive as more powerful because we fear reprisal. In any system, there is a jockeying for power between the more powerful and the less powerful. The rules in a system—formal, informal, and implicit—are made by, and tend to favor, the dominant majority whether that majority is described by race, gender, sexual preference, or doctrinal persuasion.

Furthermore, every system tends to find a power equilibrium or balance. When the balance is not egalitarian—when some have more privilege than others—dissatisfaction and conflict, overt or covert, always occurs. Just as the relative size, shape, and weight of the elements in a mobile determine the way they hang and the speed at which they move in relation to other elements, in a similar manner relative power and its corollary, fear affect the relationships of persons in a social system.

The Picture Is Not the Person:
The Family Projection System

The family projection system also muddies the picture of relationship and determines the movement of the system. As we know from the study of family systems and psychodynamic psychotherapy, one's relationship with one's parents and other significant family members, including early childhood caretakers employed by the family, impacts on the way we interact with our peers and eventually with our marital partner or significant other, should we choose one. These interactions are again strongly effected by who we perceive as more or less powerful in the family.

When an acquaintance in some way resembles one or more of the powerful caretakers in our family (such as father/mother/sister/brother/nanny/etc.), we tend to make, quite unconsciously, *assumptions* about that person based on our experience with our family member. This is called *projective identification*. The resemblance can be physical, but more likely it will be in the form of a mannerism, a tone of voice, or simply have to do with their relative place in the hierarchy of which both they and we are a part. So, for instance, if in an individual's family of origin, Father was a punitive and somewhat scary authoritarian figure, that individual might tend to always be obedient to authority—never questioning his or her boss, the committee chairperson, the minister, or the rabbi. Even more so, if Father always raised his eyebrow or his voice before he hit the individual, that person might feel uncomfortable and even threatened in the presence of a person who tends to raise an eyebrow or the voice when talking.

In another example, Mother may have always gotten her way through the covert use of power, by emotionally withdrawing from persons in the family who went against her wishes or maybe by not talking to them for a while. This is a frequently practiced and particularly powerful action. The Amish people use this form of withdrawal, called shunning, to discipline members of their community who have broken the rules. Persons who are being shunned are treated by the community as if they do not exist. An adult child from a family that used emotional withdrawal to enforce its rules might become panicked every time he or she perceived that an acquaintance was unhappy with their relationship.

This latter reaction is called abandonment anxiety and is one of the primary fears of humankind. Due to the extended vulnerability and powerlessness of the human infant as compared with other infant animals, which can stand minutes after birth and run within hours, abandonment by the parental caretaker equals death. This primitive imprint remains with most of us for life.

Finally, the projection process can be stimulated by such seemingly insignificant things as the smell of someone's aftershave or the smell of alcohol on the breath. If a person were traumatized during childhood by an alcoholic or someone who wore a certain perfume or used a particular brand of aftershave, that individual may tend to avoid or feel anxious around persons that drink or wear those scents because they are intuitively afraid of being harmed.

These projections are assumptions we make about other people. Like implicit rules, they are usually not part of our conscious awareness. They may or may not be a reflection of reality or of who the person really is. Nor are these assumptions necessarily accurate predictions of another's behavior. Sometimes our projections are on the money. Oftentimes they are not. Most important, however, it is our perception of the other, accurate or inaccurate as it might be, as well as our beliefs regarding their relative power, that influences the way we interact in a relationship and move in the system.

THE IMPACT OF HISTORY

You Were There: Assumptions Based on Past Experience

As the mobile spins through time, it accumulates wear and tear. Its pivot points become worn, its connective strands distressed, and its shiny elements dull with dust and oxidation. Without repair and renovation, its movement slows or wobbles as do all human systems with the passage of the seasons. As creatures we are the sum total of our experience. We have a habit of assuming that if a certain thing happened under certain circumstances, when those circumstances reoccur, so will the event. This phenomenon manifests with environmental happenings as well as with the interpersonal experiences just described. In its best form, this type of learning has survival value (for example, the person who has had his or her house demolished by a tornado and now hurries for a basement shelter when certain kinds of clouds appear on the horizon). In its worst form, these learnings limit our way of being in the world.

A common example is the persons who have lived through the Great Depression. These individuals often tend to be very wary of even slight economic downturns, and overly cautious about their spending. They may also have a tendency to hoard or accumulate money, and deny themselves and their families reasonable pleasures. This is because they expect or make the assumption that even though everything appears all right, disaster is just around the bend, as it was in 1929.

Communities have similar memories and expectations. In fact, many systemic rules often result from environmental insults. Formal rules regarding the management and regulation of banks and the trading of securities arose from the experience of the Great Depression. Informal and implicit rules also came into being. Common, informal rules that emerged in many families were, "Don't spend money on anything frivolous," or "Save everything." We discuss later, and in more detail, the many implicit rules that resulted from this catastrophe, but a common examples are, "You have to take care of yourself," and "Don't trust the good times—disaster is right around the corner."

Within communities, the tendency to assume that similar circumstances will produce similar results, limits a community's freedom of behavior and often prevents growth and rejuvenation. This is because individuals and groups tend to resort to the known way that the situation had been handled in the past, rather than actively choose from a number of other, possibly better, although unproven, possibilities.

It's All in the Family: The Replication of Childhood History

Finally, as was mentioned earlier, all of us, most without being aware of it, replicate our early-childhood history our family of origin experience, in every group we are part of, whether it be our marriages and families of procreation, our work environment, our social organizations, or our religious community. We do it by making, modeling, and obeying rules that were present in the families in which we grew up, and we do it by unconsciously assuming that certain traits and patterns of behavior belong to persons that in some way remind us of significant others from our childhood. To the extent that we do these things, we re-create the patterns of behavior that existed in our families when we were young. A human system operates not only as a function of its original structure, power equilibrium, and internal perceptions but also as a direct result of its experience of corporate historic events.

THE RELIGIOUS INSTITUTION AS A FAMILY SYSTEM

A Definition of Community

Congregations are not just a system; they are a particular kind of system, that which we call a community. A community is a group of people that holds something in common. As defined by the *Random House Unabridged Dictionary,* a community may be "(1) a social group of any size whose members reside in a specific locality, share government, and have a common cultural and historic heritage, *(2)* a social group sharing common characteristics or interests and perceived or perceiving itself as distinct in some respect from the larger society within which it exists, and (3) a group of men and/or women leading a common life according to a rule."[5]

All of these definitions have historically applied to communities of faith, although in today's mobile and pluralistic society the members of congregations may be sharing less and less cultural and historic heritage. They may also be finding it more and more difficult to find the boundary between themselves and society at large, and their rule of life may become poorly articulated. Mission and spiritual discipline, however, are the subjects of yet other books. At least for the moment, we can say that religious institutions see themselves as communities because their members share the history of a religious tradition. Christians, for example, see themselves in the world but not of the world and at least attempt to practice the rule of life that Jesus taught. This rule may be summed up in the Great Commandment of the Hebrew and Christian faiths; *Love the Lord your God with all your heart and with all your soul and with all your strength and with all your mind; and your neighbor as yourself* (LK10:27).

The "Family" of Faith

Even beyond being a community, congregations most often see themselves as a family, which is a particular sort of community. The word "family" comes from the Latin *familia*, meaning household. In the early history of Christianity, congregations gathered in small units called house churches. Meetings were literally held in members' houses, and the head of the household, be it man or woman, officiated at the remembrance meal called Communion or Eucharist. At present, although many congregations are larger than these early Christian house churches, they nevertheless retain a family character. In the Jewish faith, one would be hard-pressed to separate family from the practice of religion. So many of the essential rituals, such as the bringing of the new fire, or light, on the Sabbath, are family rites practiced in the home.

As we have noted earlier, members bring to the congregation conscious and unconscious patterns of behavior and rules or "family messages" that they acquired from their own families. As the religious community evolves over time, it develops a history that is similar to the history developed by a family. The sum total of this history is called the *family of origin*, a combination of family roots, tradition, and experience all rolled up into one. What have now become congregational behavior patterns are passed from elder to younger member, generation to generation, throughout the life of the religious community.

Furthermore, just as in ordinary families, important or traumatic events in the life of the congregation, such as the events of its formation, the sudden loss of a beloved leader, or clergy sexual misconduct, place an indelible stamp on the community's history. This causes the body to act and react in predictable ways when similar circumstances occur. Congregations born in conflict may always be conflicted, or the opposite, so terrified of conflict that they become paralyzed and unable to grow. Congregations that have experienced the loss of a leader and are unable to resolve their grief, may keep searching for an identical replacement, firing one clergyperson after another because he or she somehow doesn't fit the bill. Congregations that live under the cloud of clergy sexual misconduct develop a history of distrust, both of clergy and of protective lay leadership. They also develop rules regarding secrecy as well as a sense of hopelessness on the part of victims. As with every other family, the family of faith can be subject to the inter-generational transmission of sorrows.

Loyalty: A Tie That Binds

Congregations, similar to families, also become bound by ties of loyalty.[6] We usually think of loyalty as the obligation to help a friend, a family, or a community member, particularly if that person is in trouble. Indeed, loyalty ties often cause the members of a group or family to elevate group needs and values above those of the individual member. Loyalty is a survival resource for the community as a whole.

However, there is a downside as well as an upside to loyalty. These ties also allow a family or church community to tolerate the abuse of one or more of its members in the service of what it considers to be the greater goal, such as the retention of a pastor who is considered to be a great preacher or the desire to stay true to the family anticonflict rule, "Don't rock the boat."

While we most often perceive loyalty as a freely chosen virtue, all families have ways of enforcing loyalty, usually by threat of punishment. One of the most coercive punishments is that of isolation or ostracism, similar to the "shunning" discussed earlier. This sort of abandonment is tantamount to, or has the feelings of death for a young child in a family. For a member of a religious community, ostracism or abandonment can result in spiritual death, as the religious community may be the only place that the individual may be able to express and experience his or her relationship with God. Peace at all cost, is costly.

THE CONGREGATION AS A MARRIAGE

Across a Crowded Room: The Chemistry of Attraction

The Christian Church has long considered itself the Bride of Christ, so the metaphor of marriage is not new to it. Particularly interesting, however, is the marriage-like phenomenon that occurs between clergy and congregations in all denominations, Christian and Jewish alike, that court their clergy through a search process, rather than having them appointed to their positions by a denominational executive. Like marital partners, these clergy-congregational partners seek each other out for reasons that they believe are conscious and rational, yet the driving agenda is usually unconscious and emotional.

A clergyperson may consciously choose a congregation because it is located in a town or city with an excellent school system for his or her children, because the congregation is larger than the last one and represents a step up, or because the style of the congregation promises a change of pace. A congregation may choose a clergyperson because he or she is a good preacher, or because the candidate has a good bedside manner and is reputed to be a good pastor, or because he or she espouses the kind of theology with which the congregation is comfortable. This is similar to the way we think about potential spouses. Is she good-looking? Does he have a good job, or is she capable of steady employment? Will he be a good father? Will she be a good listener? Can he cook? Can she handle the finances?

What we have known for a long time about marriages, however, and for a shorter time have realized about clergy-congregational couples, is that the most important reasons for our getting together are out of our conscious awareness. Instead, God seems to bring us together to work out issues that are unresolved in our families of origin. We pair up to resolve difficulties that somehow hamper us from becoming whole. Oddly enough, we come together in committed relationships to learn to speak up for ourselves, to learn that it is all right to do tasks that we had been told were off limits, to learn to be angry, to learn that it is okay to feel sad, to learn that we do have self-worth, to learn that it is all right to be taken care of, and even to learn that we have a right to be. Like Jessica Tandy in the movie *Driving Miss Daisy*, we come together to learn that we have choices that we didn't think were there.

In *committed* relationships we can take the risk of pushing against our partner and trying out new behaviors that we were afraid to chance as children. And in so doing we grow up and grow into God. We can do this because we have *covenanted* with our partner *not to abandon us in the process*.

Growing Through Pain

Of course, in today's world of no-fault divorce, the potential of the commitment is considerable lessened. That is not to say that no-fault divorce, or divorce in general, is necessarily bad. Both partners have to be willing to work at a relationship in order for it to be tolerable, even nurturing. Marriage is very hard work, because the flip side of the coin is that we will inevitably choose partners who will constantly confront us with our difficult places, *so that the opportunity to grow will always be in front of us*.

We will pick partners who will insist on a one-up authoritarian position, who will make unilateral decisions, and who will insist upon rigid role-definitions that press us to own our power, make known our needs, and stand our ground. We will pick partners who will be afraid of feelings so that we will be forced to express ours. We will pick partners who will be overdependent so that in our exhaustion we will be made to look at the way we overfunction. We will pick partners who will deny our self-worth so that in order to survive we must define our sense of personal value. Sometimes in highly abusive relationships we will even pick partners that will deny our right to be. Statistics indicate that in many if not most battering relationships, the battering began before the partners were married! These partners press us to affirm that we, also, "are a child of the universe, no less than the trees and the stars."[7]

Because human beings never change when they are comfortable, we intuitively pick what will become uncomfortable situations that will prod us to grow. When we have done our growing, however, we no longer need the goad, and it is time for our partner to change also.

The Developmental Evolution
of the Clergy-Congregational Partnership

Clergy-congregational partners face the same sort of difficult grace.
Both clergy and congregation choose one another for their ability to
constantly make present the "old business" that each needs to grow
through so that together they become a whole and more holy community. For example, some clergypersons are insecure and have a need to
control their environment. This may be because in their family of
origin the environment was chaotic and emotionally volatile and
always falling apart, or the situation was scary and physical or emotional survival depended on having control over what was going on.
Family systems in which there is physical, emotional, sexual, or substance abuse fall into this category.

Insecure clergy will have a tendency to need to be in control, to be
in charge, and to be one-up. These clergypersons may pick a congregation in which the balance of power is toward the laity so that
they are always in a control struggle. The clergyperson has come to
the congregation and through the process of interaction learns that
letting go of control is all right and does not equal death. He or she
may need to learn how to partner and share power.

The congregation, on the other hand, may have historically
decided that bad things happen when they are not in charge. Perhaps
they once had a minister that misappropriated funds. Or maybe the
leadership of the congregation is made up of persons that are used to
making unilateral decisions, either because that is how they operate
in the business world, or because key figures come from families
that have an authoritarian structure where perhaps the father makes
all the important decisions. A good example is the sizable New
England United Church of Christ congregation that was controlled
by a single layleader for fifty years. A banker and school board
chairperson, he served lifetime terms on both the Board of Deacons
and the Board of Trustees, determined their agendas, and dismissed
the meetings if they took a turn not to his liking!

These congregations may be intuitively hoping to learn how to
trust their ordained leaders, how to let go, and how to become a
partnership. In some ways they have been working too hard, and
need to learn how to let themselves be cared for. As long as both the

congregation and the clergyleader battle for control, clergy tenure will probably be very short, as one "divorce" after another takes place, and not having worked through the issue, the problem repeats itself. The congregation cited above had some ministers that lasted only two weeks!

Most times, growing requires taking apart our assumptions, even our treasured ones, about other persons in order to discover who they really are. It also requires discovering those parts of our own selves that we have denied or kept out of consciousness. This is somewhat similar to the worn mobile that must be disassembled in order to be refurbished. The awareness gained through this dismantling may be painful, but it allows us to grown into real relationships. Edwin Friedman, a rabbi and noted family therapist, has said that the capacity to tolerate pain equals the ability to grow. Paul the Apostle wrote, "suffering produces endurance, and endurance produces character, and character produces hope, and hope does not disappoint us because God's love has been poured into our hearts through the Holy Spirit" (Rom 5:3-5).

The Shepherd and the Sheep: Parent-Child versus Co-Workers in Faith

Another aspect of marriage is the tendency to develop a pattern of leader and follower or of parent and child instead of two equal peers. One of the common biblical metaphors of the Christian faith is that of shepherds and sheep. "I am the good shepherd. The good shepherd lays down his life for the sheep" (Jn 10:11). The metaphor is about caring and sacrifice a good descriptor of ethical living. Unfortunately, it is often misinterpreted in the religious context to mean that the clergyleader is the all powerful guide and unilateral decision maker, and the rest of the community should become disempowered, dumb followers.

The pattern for partnership that is set down in scripture is that of two *helpmates*—a term that denotes mutual support but not unilateral domination. Adam and Eve were to be peers, cocreators with God, working side by side in God's garden. Congregational systems, however, frequently fail to become egalitarian partnerships, which is the real goal of marriage. Instead they develop into an uneven hierarchy where the clergy-congregational "marriage" becomes similar to a parent-child relationship. Certainly this is not what Jesus of Nazareth had in mind when he spoke the pastoral metaphor just quoted.

Communities that have insecure, controlling clergy with poor self-esteem, similar to the example above, matched with a membership that does not have a sense of its own competence are at risk for the development of the parent-child dynamic. These are congregations that have not discovered the concept of the "priesthood of all believers." This commission, first from the words of Moses in Exodus 19:6, "but you [the Israelite people] shall be for me a priestly kingdom and a holy nation" is then echoed in the letter of 1Peter, *"But you are a chosen race, a royal priesthood, a holy nation, God's own people, in order that you may proclaim the mighty acts of him who called you out of darkness into his marvelous light"* (1Pet 2:9). This commission gives the responsibility of right living and evangelism to the entire community, not only to the priest, the minister, or the rabbi.[8]

Inherent in parent-child relationships are expectations and behaviors that give the clergyperson the power to make all the rules, and then by default, shoulder all the responsibility. The "parent" becomes the lonely guide who is also supposed to do all the caring and be ultimately accountable for the well-being of the "family." This is not only a terrible burden on the clergy, but it also teaches the congregation *learned incompetence*, that is, the sense that they are not capable of decision making or even performance. Then, when things do not go right, the congregation, not surprisingly, blames or scapegoats the clergy. Such a congregation will quickly become apathetic, unsupportive, and underfunctioning, while the clergyperson burns out.

SUMMARY

In summation, religious communities function in many ways like family systems. Their internal dynamics are structured by formal, informal, and implicit rules that arise through evolutionary processes and/or are brought to the community from the individual backgrounds of its members.

Issues of power, born of the struggle to survive, affect the dynamics of the system. Power, be it position or status, is the ability to influence an outcome. An advantage of this sort provides at least an illusion of security, and its corollary, fear, becomes a significant determinant in human relationships.

The family projection process—the tendency of persons to make assumptions about the character and behavior of others and to act accordingly—also affects the dynamics of the religious system. Projective identification is the unconscious merging of the characteristics of a person from our past (usually a significant caretaker) with an acquaintance in our present. We fail to really "see" the immediate individual but instead behave as if we were in a relationship with that specter from an earlier time. Community members bring to the congregation not only their family rules or "messages," but also their projective assumptions, expectations, and behavioral patterns.

The history of events that the community experiences as a unit also affects the way it functions. Dysfunctional systemic rules often result from environmental insults such as the loss of a significant person, relationship, or vocation, for example, and clergy misconduct. The tendency of communities to assume that similar circumstances will produce similar results, limits a community's freedom of behavior and often prevents growth and rejuvenation.

Congregations are also bound by ties of loyalty, which cause the membership to elevate group needs and values above that of the individual members. While loyalty is a survival resource for the community as a whole, it can also cause the family of faith to tolerate the abuse of individuals in the service of the system.

Finally, the clergy-congregational partnership in many denominations has many qualities of a marriage, which when healthy enables both the clergyperson and the congregation to become whole as each challenges the other's "old business." When unhealthy, this partnership disintegrates into a parent-child relationship, which may lead to disempowerment, burnout, abuse, abandonment, and divorce.

Chapter 2

The Illusion of Eden and the Fortified City

Desert travelers are familiar with the phenomenon of the mirage. Shimmering heat waves rising from the sunbaked sand create the optical illusion of a lake of water. This illusion is then often transformed in the mind of the parched wanderer to a paradise of pools and palm trees, a life-sustaining oasis in the wilderness. Likewise, members of religious institutions often participate in the wishful illusion that the congregation is the perfect family of God—perhaps the perfect family that they did not experience as a child. The Christian Church in particular has always represented itself as creating the "kingdom (of God) among us" thereby implying that it is in this community that we recreate paradise on earth. Our hunger for this perfect family is destined to be frustrated. Many congregations, however, attempt to maintain their dream by avoiding conflict at all costs and by building about themselves inner and outer walls of denial, rationalization, and repression.

A LACK OF EMOTIONAL NOURISHMENT AND THE HUNGER TO BE FILLED

Human families are rarely perfect. As we have seen in the preceding chapter, fear and insecurity create all sorts of destructive behavioral patterns that are passed, mostly unconsciously, from generation to generation through modeling. One of the important consequences of dysfunction is emotional emptiness. When we are infants, most generally we are held when we are fed, be it by breast or bottle. As a result, physical nurturance—in this case, milk—and emotional nurturance, that of being held and comforted, become closely associated in the child's mind, an experience that persists into adulthood. Correspondingly, a lack of emotional nourishment takes on the aspect of physical starvation[1] and leads to emotional emptiness. When parents, for whatever reason, are not able to nurture their children emotionally, these children grow up emotionally hungry, starved for attention, affirmation, and love.

There are many causes of deficient parenting. Putting aside the more obvious situations in which psychosis[2] or personality disorder[3] exist, the most common causes of disabled parenting are poverty and grief. In a market-driven economy such as ours, material poverty often leads to spiritual poverty, anger, and resentment that is often displaced on the more vulnerable persons in intimate relationships, particularly on children. Grief, on the other hand, often causes emotional withdrawal or distancing, as the grieving person turns inward for understanding and solace and away from significant others in the immediate environment. Grief can come from many causes including, but not limited to, the loss of a loved one. Grief can also result from the loss of a job or vocation, a divorce, an abortion or miscarriage, or even geographic relocation to a strange neighborhood or a nursing home away from friends and familiar surroundings.

In the example of the Great Depression, this environmental insult brought both poverty and grief together and placed a deep scar in the psyches of North Americans that crossed racial and economic boundaries. Many families lost their life's savings and even livelihoods. Parental energy was focused on simple survival and entrapped in overwhelming grief over the loss of all for which they had labored. The pain was so unbearable that once economically comfortable and powerful people committed suicide. Emotional and physical resources were stretched to the limit as young and old competed for a severely diminished number of jobs that involved working long hours for scanty pay. People were tired and angry and hopeless. There was little emotional support or physical comfort left to lavish on the children.

A "Good Enough" Holding Environment

D. W. Winnicott, a pediatrician and renowned developmental psychologist and child analyst, birthed the concept of the "good enough" holding environment—an environment in which an infant feels wholly supported, both physically and emotionally, by its primary caretakers. He considered that if an infant had a "good enough" holding environment, the infant would evolve as a psychologically healthy individual—secure, trusting, and competent in relationship abilities. Securely held in the caretaker's arms, with its physical and emotional needs regularly and predictably attended to, the infant learns to trust in the "goodness" of its environment. This trust is the foundation upon which is based the capacity to take risks, such as letting go of the mother's hand and taking the first few unsteady steps, unaided, across the room. Later on, this "holding" takes the form of affirmations from the caretakers with respect to the young child's competence and value. As a result, the child develops inner direction, or an "inner yardstick," and a sense of self-worth. The capacity to trust in the goodness of the environment—one that provides ready support when needed, while at the same time giving permission for the evolving person to be separate—is proportional to the potential for personal growth, self-realization, and ultimate happiness.

In depleted or empty families such as those of the Depression, children are seen as burdens. As a result, they are taught that they are not to have needs and that they are not to express or sometimes even feel want of anything. Often children are inappropriately expected to emotionally, sometimes even physically, care for their parents rather than the reverse. Instead of the parent comforting the child in trying circumstances, the opposite occurs. Five-year-olds worry about the budget and getting their clothes dirty, and ten-year-olds patiently listen to one parent's complaint about the other, working hard to make mommy and daddy happy, which is an impossible task. Children are assigned all the responsibility for the emotional welfare of the family without any of the power. They learn that they are displeasing, especially when they require attention, and that when bad things happen it is all their fault. In family therapy lingo we say that the children are "parentified," meaning that the family hierarchy is reversed.

Needless to say, this is an unhappy situation. Those of us that grow up in such an environment long for attention, affection, and affirmation. We want to be told that we are good and valuable. We want a family that can receive us, "hold" us, and nurture us. And these are the promises of religious institutions, that is, as long as we play by the rules.

FAITH, BELIEF, TRUST, COMMITMENT, AND THE HOPE OF SECURITY

Ever since our expulsion from Eden, trust, for human beings, has been a very big word. Having given up faith in a provident God and now believing that we must rely solely on our own resources, one of our greatest difficulties is having to live with uncertainty. As a result, we search for something we can know and hold on to. Whether it is the serious uncertainty of whether or not we will have food for dinner tonight, a job tomorrow, or what will happen at our physical death, or minor uncertainties such as what people will think of us and our behavior, most of us have a tendency to spend a lot of time trying to make the unknown knowable.

Living the Question

Faith, as opposed to belief (which is a certainty), is the process of learning to love and even to live the questions of our lives while trusting that because we are held in the arms of God, it will be all right. The well-known poet, Rainer Maria Rilke wrote:

> have patience with everything unresolved in your heart and try to love the *questions themselves* as if they were locked rooms or books written in a very foreign language. Don't search for the answers, which could not be given to you now, because you would not be able to live them. And the point is, to live everything. *Live* the questions now. Perhaps then, someday far in the future, you will gradually, without even noticing it, live your way into the answer.[4]

Rilke's point is that the *process* we go through to discover the answer is much more important than the final discovery itself. The journey of faith is, as a famous, though anonymous fourteenth century author put it, one of stepping into the "cloud of unknowing." The difficulty, of course, is that when we enter the process we cannot know the outcome. Indeed, if we did, the outcome might seem so terrifying and the process so arduous that we would never undertake it. Witness Moses' reluctance to embark upon the task of bringing his people out of Egypt and the Israelite's complaints in the desert. Yet it is in this very process, this experiment in living, that we develop the resources to sustain our new way of being. We come to know our strengths and our weaknesses, we learn that we can take a risk and survive. It is like learning to walk again but this time in a new way. We learn to trust again. We learn to love. Living the question *is* the spiritual life. Faith is trusting that it will be all right.

At their best, religious institutions are the adult environment that provides the opportunity for persons to embark upon this journey and be nurtured in transit. They are a space where we can share the precious secrets of our souls. At their worst, instead of a being a holding environment that liberates, religious institutions become a thoughtful prison of dogma and prejudice that locks us in while locking others out. That discussion, however, is beyond the scope of this work. Nonetheless, throughout the history of humankind, from our earliest tribal gatherings to the present day New Age fellowships, it is within communities of *faith*, however they are constituted, that persons have learned what it is to be fully human.

The Right Hand of Fellowship

One of the venerable rituals of induction into a religious community is the extension of the right hand of fellowship, given after the prospective member has vowed commitment to the family of faith. This ancient transaction predates biblical times but is first recorded in scripture when God covenants with Noah "that never again shall all flesh be cut off by the waters of a flood, and never again shall there be a flood to destroy the earth (Gn 9:11, NRSV). The covenant is a binding agreement made between parties and in the sight of God, in which the community and the prospective member agree to support one another. Indeed, the word *religion*, itself, comes from the Latin verb *religare*, which means to tie or bind.

We hope, of course, in that being so bound, we will not be abandoned during our spiritual struggle on the stormy waters of uncertainty. We hope that this is a place where we can allow ourselves to be seen and received for who we really are. We hope, although perhaps unawares, that here, at last, we will not be abandoned in our intimate relationships during those moments that we make ourselves the most vulnerable. We hope that here at last we will be held fast.

THE FEAR OF CONFLICT

Try as we might to persuade ourselves, however, we know intuitively that covenants between people are more fragile than covenants with the Godhead. And we have learned in our families of origin that conflict often results in pain, loss, and abandonment, or at least emotional abandonment. Losers lose *out*. So, paradoxically, in our communities of faith, which we perceive as our last bastion of safety, we avoid conflict at all costs. We do so by ignoring problems and personal trespasses as long as possible. We may grumble about them to another, uninvolved party, which allows us to let off steam without risking confrontation, conflict, and possible retribution or rejection. We may stay silent and suffer. We may blame the problem we are having on someone else without recognizing our own part in it. But generally, religious communities subscribe to the rule "Don't rock the boat," because on some level they are afraid that the Ark will sink in the flood.

Emotional Lances

Another tacit family rule that we frequently import into congregations, which also mediates against healthy conflict resolution, is "Thou shalt not be angry." This rule often develops in families where the expression of anger has caused substantial harm, even the death of other family members. As a result, the family intuitively, and without discussion, decides that anger is dangerous and must not be expressed or perhaps not even felt! Anger, however, is a fundamental human emotion with significant survival value. It cannot be eradicated. It can be driven underground.

It is a well-known statistic that the highest percentage of homicides occur within the context of the family structure. That is because when we live in constant intimate contact, as family members do, we become well acquainted with each other's vulnerabilities or sensitive spots. We know where the scale is missing in the dragon's armor. Unfortunately, when family members are angry with one another, they often have the graceless habit of throwing emotional lances at the intimate other with whom they are unhappy. Such lances a intuitively home in on these unprotected places. An example of this would be the wife, who is frustrated with her husband's shyness and lack of desire for social involvement. In her pique, she remarks, "I suppose it doesn't matter. No one would enjoy your company anyway." This might seem only a little hard at the outset, but in this case, the husband happened to have been born out of wedlock, a bastard. He had been told by his mother that his birth had ruined her prospective career, that his being was a burden, and that his presence, his *company* was not enjoyable. This was a big, unresolved sore spot—his sense of worthlessness *and of being unlovable*. It was the reason he was shy. His wife, of course, was aware that he had been born out of wedlock. Unfortunately, she was not a psychotherapist, and did not understand the full import of the consequences of his birth. In fact, neither did her husband. They only both knew that he was shy and hated to go to parties or any social functions, which for the wife was a real drag. Her words, however, were aimed at a place where they would not fall on deaf ears. She gets a result, though not what she really wanted. Instead of drawing forth a reluctant agreement to go to the party, her words detonate an explosion similar to an atom bomb.

Paradoxically, families that suppress anger are more in danger of lethal explosions, than families that get it out and get it over with. The metaphor of the volcano is a useful one. When heat and pressure are contained below layers of rock, they have the opportunity to build up until the consolidated energy blows through its restraints, spewing rock, ash, gas and fiery lava over a wide area totally decimating it. Likewise, when emotional pressure builds up, its release can be devastating. On the other hand, small releases, such as the daily spouting of a hot spring geyser, stabilize the pressure so that its discharge is not harmful. Religious institutions, unfortunately, are more similar to the volcano than the geyser.

Our culture gives anger a bad name. In fact, consciously channeled anger is the energy of change. Certainly even Jesus of Nazareth recognized that change cannot occur without conflict. Someone, usually in the minority faction, must become dissatisfied with the status quo and push for a transformation. This is what Martin Luther King did. One might say he was an angry man; however, he was a man with a purpose. Change never comes about when everyone is happy, and pushing for change creates conflict.

Ironically, the life of faith is all about change and the shattering of one's illusions. Unfortunately, religious communities are more resistant to change and recognizing and dealing with the corresponding conflict than any other human institution. Instead, we have the tendency to tenaciously cling to our fantasy of the happy family where everything is the same and nothing can go wrong.

THE FORTIFIED CITY: THE PUBLIC FACE OF PROSPERITY THAT HIDES THE PRIVATE FACE OF POVERTY

Conflicted, dysfunctional families, perhaps because of the lack of inner direction, low self-esteem, and the need of external affirmation of their members, tend to be particularly sensitive to public opinion. As a result, they make a special effort to present a family front that portrays themselves as happy, healthy, and upstanding members of the community. A not-uncommon scenario is the family that attended church not only every Sunday, but also on all the high holy days. The householders were considered sustaining members of the congregation. The children, however, were regularly sexually abused by the paternal grandfather, paternal cousin, the father, and two maternal uncles. No one suspected it. In another family the father is a well-known lawyer much admired for his public service. Out in the world he is a philanthropist. At home he beats his children. When questioned, the children lie about how they received their bruises, saying that they fell downstairs or had some other accident. In a third family, the children are late to school and receive detentions. They do not tell their teacher that they were late because they had to clean the vomit off their alcoholic mother, pick her up off the floor, and put her to bed.

Persons in these types of families simply lower their heads and keep on pulling the load. They are also usually taught to deny the reality around them and believe the improbable or even the impossible.

Highly Defended Families: The Outer Walls

Families of this sort are very private and have difficulty accepting help, rarely allowing others to see what really goes on inside.

They commonly have the informal family rule, "We take care of our own." Problems such as alcoholism and abuse are minimized or denied by both the perpetrators and the victims. Mental illness may be seen as shameful and kept covered up. Even money problems are publicly denied, and needed assistance is refused or left unsought. Children may be discouraged from bringing friends home to play, and family loyalty to the rule of secrecy is fierce. These families are called *highly defended* because they maintain a protective wall themselves to ward off societal judgment in the same way that ancient cities were walled in order to ward off possible invaders.

Highly Defended Persons: The Inner Walls

Individuals who come from families such as these also build inner walls around themselves. All of us have ways of protecting ourselves from realities that are too harsh to bear. In psych-speak we call these *ego defense mechanisms*. Persons from highly defended families make particular use of the defense mechanisms of *denial, rationalization*, and *repression*. Denial is the process of convincing oneself that what is happening is not really happening. The alcoholic, born of an empty childhood, who tells herself that she is not abusing alcohol because she only consumes one six-pack of beer every evening, is using denial.

Rationalization is the process of convincing oneself of the goodness of something harmful. The emotionally immature pedophile who tells himself that nothing is wrong and that the five-year-old enjoyed the encounter because she had an orgasm when he sexually abused her, is using rationalization.

Repression is the process of forcefully forgetting part of one's experience. The sexually abused five-year-old who grows up believing she is a virgin, but has panic attacks and an inability to achieve orgasm when she makes love to her new husband, is using repression. The Vietnam veteran who has a sleep disorder, is doing "recreational" drugs and alcohol, and for years tells himself that he's just taking a little deserved time off before he gets a job and gets on with his life, is using all three defense mechanisms.

Individuals who use denial, rationalization, and repression are not bad. In fact, the events in their lives may indeed have been, or even still are, so terrible that protecting themselves in this way is the only way they can survive emotionally, at least without additional resources. Unfortunately, however, these defenses prevent the awareness that might allow these persons to grow through their trauma, depression, and feelings of guilt. These defenses also become old, bad habits and are easily applied to all new, uncomfortable situations, creating a downward spiral into despair.

Highly Defended Congregations

Congregations are also often highly defended with fortifications that go beyond the protection and nurturance of theological perceptions. This is because communities of faith are supposed to mirror the holy, and being holy is a significant image to maintain. Religious institutions usually prefer to be seen as fortresses against the ravages of the world and places where everything is right and peaceful. But even beyond that, the members of the congregation really want to believe that nothing is wrong. They need to believe in order to maintain not only the comforting illusion of Eden but also that of the perfect family. This of course is a form of denial.

A telling example of this sort of defensiveness came with the publishing of the book, *Congregation: The Journey Back to Church* by Gary Dorsey.[5] An exceedingly well-written and poignant look into the ordinary workings of a New England United Church of Christ congregation, Dorsey's work was severely criticized by numbers of parish members. "Some called me an SOB and a rapist," Dorsey was quoted as saying in an article in the United Church News.[6] Actually, what Dorsey created, by immersing himself in daily congregational life, was a chronicle of "the scut work of day-to-day religious life," as well as vibrant portraits of committed people of God, lay and clergy alike, in a mainline, landmark church of 1,100 members. What he also created was his own transformation from observer to participant in a place where he found "wonder was familiar." Yet, some of the members felt that "they had been betrayed and exposed" by the telling of the story. These members felt their community had been seen, without permission, by outsiders (the book's readers) and that what had come to light was not as perfect as they would have had it. It is here that secrecy and confidentiality become confused, an issue that we shall take up later in Chapter 6.

In other familiar examples, individual religious communities will struggle for decades, even centuries, with recurrent problems, but unlike a floundering business, never avail themselves of a consultant. Partly this is due to the unwillingness of certain factions, in some cases the clergypersons themselves, to give up control to an outside person. This tends to hole true in some denominations more frequently than in others. Most of the time, however, there simply is an unwillingness to admit that something is really wrong and that the "family" does not have sufficient resources of its own to fix it. The recent epidemic of exposés of clergy sexual misconduct is in part a direct result of this sort of protectionism. Because religious institutions have not wished to confront or even recognize the problem, they have not developed the appropriate resources to confront the scourge of misconduct. But since we have come into a new age where sexual abuse can be talked about, victims have discovered that they have voices,[7] and the courts have come into the picture to balance the scales of justice. Institutional denial, just like family denial, always compounds the problem by allowing the injury to reach greater depths. As with an unattended and festering wound, when more people are hurt for a longer time, healing becomes very complicated.

GOD IN THE GARDEN: THE IDOLIZATION OF THE SPIRITUAL LEADER

Finally, it seems important to mention one more thing. Religious bodies have a tendency to iconize their leaders, to set them on a pillar and turn them into gods, which heightens the illusion of Eden. Rabbi Jack Bloom, also a clinical psychologist, called this process the creation of the *symbolic exemplar*. We do this because we want to believe that our pastor embodies all the wonderful things that we feel we cannot be, or all the wonderful things that our parents could not be. We want to imagine that our pastor is the unstinting caretaker that will never abandon us, never hurt us, never do wrong by us, and always protect us, leading us beside the still waters of safety and security. There is a part of us that wants to be a sheep and let the shepherd do all the hard work. That of course is not what discipleship is all about. Nor is it possible for any human being, however gifted, to be God, Abraham, Mohammed, or Jesus Christ, for that matter. Eventually, if not simply out of exhaustion to live up to our expectations, our hero will fail. At first we may deny that such an event could or is happening and that is the subject of the next chapter. But when he or she finally crashes to the floor from such a great height and our illusions are at last shattered, we usually become very frightened and then, because fear itself is too scary, we quickly replace the fear with anger and a feeling of betrayal. To avoid this tragedy it is especially important that we see our ordained clergy as whole persons, as combinations of strength and weakness, of light and darkness. We should see them as sinners, such as we all are, and as saints, but now counting ourselves among them.

SUMMARY

Out of their need for love, affirmation, and approval, the members of religious communities have a tendency to create the illusion that their congregation is the perfect family of God, perhaps unlike the families in which they grew up. Unfortunately, Eden has left us, or at least we chose to leave it. Instead, we find ourselves in the desert. As individuals we forget that living water only comes from deep spiritual wells that are the hard work of awareness.

Our hunger to be emotionally filled and our fears of uncertainty lead us to substitute fantasy for faith. Because we long to be bound and held in loving arms, and because we are afraid of abandonment and intuitively aware of the frailty of human covenants, as members of congregations we avoid conflict and confrontation within the community. Because we give anger a bad name, we do not harness its energy to enable constructive change. We also want to believe that nothing is or can be wrong. In so doing, we become blind to behavior that threatens the health of the congregation, thus creating a highly defended family system.

Finally, in our desire for the perfect nurturing parent, in our families of faith we have a tendency to iconize our leaders, to set them on a pillar, and to turn them into gods. This heightens the illusion of Eden, stunts congregational growth, and provides a pathway for abuse and disappointment.

Chapter 3

God Transference, the Good Object, and the Makeup of Ministers

One of the difficulties with religious systems is that we tend to turn our leaders into gods and worship them instead of that which is truly holy. In fact, we get so attached to them that we would worship even their more tangible mortal remnants, rather than the great but quite intangible *I AM*. It was in recognition of this frailty of ours that God made certain that Moses' body remained hidden after his death. And certainly Jesus confronted this same inclination when, after his resurrection, he admonished Mary Magdalene in the garden, saying, "Do not hold on to me" (Jn 20:17). It is just simpler to have a relationship, although perhaps an imaginary relationship, with another human being than it is to cultivate a relationship with the numinous. It is easier to have expectations of human persons, and it is easier to determine whether or not those expectations have been met. But, above all, most of us have a greater illusion of control over our human relationships than we have over our relationship with God.

The relationship that we would like to have the most control over is our relationship with our primary caretakers, most often our father and our mother. This is because these persons are primarily responsible for the nurturance, the emotional and physical support, that enables us to grow into competent adults. Having good parents, or having a good relationship with one's parents, has survival value. Instinctively we know that without parents or primary caretakers we would perish. And in some cases, of course, should we incur their disfavor, we might perish because of them.

Turning clergypersons into gods can be misleading, if not damaging, to individuals as well as to the congregation as a whole. Spiritual leaders are actually very human and frequently come from dysfunctional families. In addition, the very personality traits that make competent religious professionals can also lead to sexual acting out. As a group, clergy tend to be able to talk the talk better than they can walk the walk.

GOD TRANSFERENCE AND THE GOOD OBJECT

The psychology of our tendency to transfigure our religious leaders into gods can be explained by the theory of object relations. This school of psychodynamic psychotherapy was heavily influenced by Margaret Mahler (1897-1985). In psychodynamic terminology "objects" are the people to whom one is attached by strong emotional ties. According to this theory, infants tend to split their impressions or early images of their primary caretakers, primary objects,[1] into an internalized good image or *good object* and an internalized bad image or *bad object*. The *good object* image contains all the nurturing, satisfying, and comforting impressions that the infant has of the caretaker, while the *bad object* image contains all the frustrating, frightening, and depriving impressions of the caretaker. That is, in the infant mind, and to a greater or lesser extent in the adult mind, there are two separate concepts of each primary caretaker. There is a good mother/father/nanny and a bad mother/father/nanny. Hopefully, as the individual matures into adulthood, he or she begins to see each of these caretakers as an integrated whole of light and darkness.

Unfortunately, that development is frequently arrested by early childhood trauma and at its best is rarely completed until well into middle age. Instead, either the good caretaker (good object) or the bad caretaker (bad object) is repressed or at least to some degree forced out of consciousness. As a result, the adult child perceives the caretaker as one-sided—either too perfect or too imperfect, too good or too bad, a saint or a sinner. The mother/father/nanny is seen or remembered only in terms of his or her virtues or his or her faults rather than as a combination of both.

God Transference and the Frog Prince

Needless to say, it would be nice to have a perfect parent who always gave us what we wanted, loved us unconditionally, affirmed us, nurtured us and who never abandoned us, hurt us, or punished us. In short, it would be nice to have God as our parent, if only God could have warm, cuddly arms, a soft voice, and kind eyes as well. Unfortunately, human parents don't arrive in that variety, even though most of us at least on some level long for such a person most, if not all, of our lives.

Human beings, however, are programmed to survive and are usually quite creative. When we do not have what we want, most of us try to make it or at least obtain what we desire in some way. Here one might be reminded of the fairy tale called the Frog Prince.[2] In this story the proverbial young princess is playing and tossing her golden ball when it unhappily rolls into a deep well. A large, ugly frog who happens to inhabit the well hears the girl's lament and offers to retrieve it for her—for a price. Quite cheekily he asks that he be allowed to be her companion at play, at table, and even in bed in return for the ball, and quite insincerely she accords him her promise. The frog performs his part of the bargain, but the young princess reneges on hers and runs home. Eventually the frog makes his way to the castle to collect his due, and when the princess' stern father the king finds out about the mishap, he insists that she also perform what she had promised. When bedtime arrives the princess is revolted at the thought of sleeping with the frog, who threatens to tell on her if she does not comply. In her frustration, she throws the frog against the wall and he immediately turns into a prince. The two are married and the prince whisks her away from her stern father, taking her to his own castle where the two live happily ever after.

Of course all sorts of morals might be drawn from this tale, but with respect to our current interest, it is worthy to note that when the young lady is up against the wall, so to speak, the frog conveniently turns into a prince with a golden crown. When, for whatever reasons we find ourselves in what seem to be powerless positions, as was the princess who had to obey her father, many of us become creative. When we are emotionally empty or abused as a child, most often and quite unconsciously, we go about creating the perfect parent by projecting a picture of our good object, that warm, friendly, satisfying image, onto another person. This is called *transference*. We *transfer* what is really part of ourselves—our internal image of the good object—to someone else. Then, much like the Frog Prince of the fairy tale, we imagine that person has become our long-sought-after perfect parent/lover/god, the person that *can* give us all the nurturance that we are lacking. We forget to look at his or her webbed feet and see instead only the golden crown. The frog, our potential partner or our clergyperson, has become very powerfully transfigured.

Hanging on to Eden

As was mentioned in Chapter 2, the canonization of religious leaders disempowers the other members of the congregation, because the clerypersons are seen as all-powerful and all-provident, while the rest of the family of faith perceives themselves as incompetent and in need of being rescued. However, our hunger for the good object can have an even more disastrous result. *When we need to see our leaders as the perfect parent that we never had, we are willing to overlook even their gross misbehaviors in order to maintain our very dearly held illusion.* The Eden fantasy of the perfect family with the perfect parent can be very costly, especially when serious offenses such as sexual misconduct are involved. We will study this more deeply in Chapter 5.

THE MAKEUP OF MINISTERS

Most persons in the social services are fairly complex individuals, and clergy are no exception. Who is the person behind our projections, our unconscious wishful fantasies? Who is the person that we think we see but most probably do not know? As we have discussed, personality develops from a combination of our biology and our family history, the events and family rules or messages that have conditioned and guided our behavior. Biology and history combine to create personality traits, the fairly stable characteristics that frame one as a person: personality states, the transient conditions one finds oneself in, depends on the current impact of one's environment.

The Root of Jesse

Clergy, like most members of the helping professions, frequently come from dysfunctional families. In a 1988 study[3] conducted with a sample of unusually high-functioning clergy participants, of the various family stress indicators measured, 91 percent reported chronic physical dysfunction and problems with weight in their own or their spouse's family of origin, 83 percent reported chronic emotional disorder and suicide attempts, 75 percent reported diminished sexual interest and acting-out children, 66 percent reported substance abuse, 58 percent reported affairs/illegitimate children and problems with the law, 50 percent reported chronic or episodic physical violence, 25 percent reported incest, and 8 percent reported compulsive gambling. Needless to say, they did not come from perfect families, and the individuals in the sample would probably be the first to admit that they were hardly perfect themselves.

Studies[4] indicate that the clergyperson's family of origin significantly influences the way the clergyperson relates to his or her own family as well as to the congregational family.

Self-Esteem and Behavioral Scripts

Without the help of psychotherapy, family dysfunction usually leads to poor self-esteem. This is the result of a whole battery of mostly tacit family messages and scripts for behavior that are promulgated in families of this sort. Until these rules are made conscious, and the issue of family loyalties to these rules is addressed, family members, including the clergyperson, will more or less function according to these precepts. Some of the major family proscriptions[5] are:

- *Deny:* Do not think about, see, hear, feel, reflect on, or question your experience. Do not believe the obvious; accept the impossible.

- *Don't trust self or others:* Do not trust your own perceptions. Don't trust or disclose to others including your own family members (this is a way of maintaining family secrets).
- *Be loyal:* You must protect the family. You must keep the secret. You must obey. (These families are frequently authoritarian.) You must not fight back, disagree or get angry, or you will be abandoned.
- *Don't have needs:* Put the other's needs before your own. Children must *earn* attention. Don't be selfish as there is not enough to go around. *Don't be. You are unwanted and a burden* (this may be expressed in suicidal ideation).
- *Love means being hurt or used:* If you want my love, you have to give me your body. If you don't let me use your body, you don't love me.
- *Don't ask for help:* Don't betray the family secret by asking for help.
- *Don't show pain:* Don't be dramatic as it's really not that bad. Somaticize—keep it inside, deny it, don't express it—physical pain is more acceptable than emotional pain. Don't sully another person's day; don't bother me or make me feel bad.
- *Don't be a child:* Act like an adult and support your parents. Don't be curious. Don't play. Don't make mistakes. Be adult-like without the power or authority. Be responsible for everyone else.
- *It is your fault:* You are responsible for all problems. You are bad, evil, immoral, and guilty. You are responsible for the feelings and behaviors of others. Stay in control of yourself and others. Anything bad that happens is your fault, so stay on guard.
- *You are incompetent:* You are never perfect enough. Don't try it unless you can do it right. We did (gave) for you because you can't do for yourself.

These messages, common in dysfunctional families, can cause severe relational impairment. The *Deny* and *Don't trust* rules result in other-directedness, or a dependence on the perception of others. They also lead to an ultimate sense of worthlessness and interfere significantly with the capacity for intimate relationships, since the individual cannot take the risks necessary for deep personal encounters. The *Be loyal* rules prevent the individual from taking a stand in opposition to the majority opinion, and leave only the option of passive-aggressive behavior. The *Don't have needs, Don't ask for help,* and *Don't show pain* rules oppose adequate self-care and even encourage self-destructive behavior. These rules also hinder clergy from seeking out help with marital difficulties, depression, anxiety, and other similar problems. The *Love means being hurt or used* rules lead to a confusion over what love really is and to a sense of being ultimately unlovable. These rules can also lead to sexual acting out, including pedophilia or other forms of clergy sexual misconduct. The *Don't be a child* and *It is your fault* rules lead to over-responsibility and workaholism as well as a sense of shamefulness and self-hatred. They can also result in a terrible need for control. The *You are incompetent* rule enforces perfectionism even to the point of performance paralysis as a result of the fear of making a mistake. When clergy have inherited these messages from their families of origin, it affects their marriages and families of procreation as well as their congregational families.

Personality Traits as Seen Through the Lens of the Myers-Briggs Type Indicator

Over time, one's biology and one's history consolidate into certain fairly stable personality traits or behavioral signatures. Another way of looking at these signatures is through the lens of the Myers-Briggs Type Indicator,[6] a well-researched and validated inventory originally created by the mother-daughter team of Katharine Cook Briggs and Isabel Briggs Myers. This instrument utilizes the personality typology developed by Carl Jung, the first psychologist to study adult, rather than purely child, development. Jung's hypothesis was that adult development proceeds along four vectors or continuums:

Extraversion	Introversion
Sensing	Intuition
Thinking	Feeling
Judging	Perceiving

Along the first vector, or extraversion-introversion continuum, extraverts relate more to the outer world of things, people, and the environment, and their primary source of energy comes from the outside world. They are talkative, active, and easily fatigued by reading or study. Politicians who get charged up by speaking to crowds, and clergy who are energized by preaching to congregations would be examples of persons that tend toward this type.

Introverts prefer to relate more to the inner world of ideas, images, dreams, and *archetypes*, or the symbolic world. They draw their energy from within and need solitude to recharge. They may be reflective and reserved, persons of few words with few intense relationships. Jesus, Moses, and the solitary artist or mystic would be indicative of the introvert type. It is worthy to note that introverts do not necessarily dislike or avoid people. Rather, they need to withdraw in order to recontact their source of energy.

The second of Jung's vectors is the sensing-intuition continuum. Sensing individuals are data gatherers who enjoy detail. They tend to obtain information about the world through their five senses and tend to be concrete, practical, and down to earth. Medical practitioners and laboratory scientists are examples of this type.

Intuitives, on the other hand, obtain their information from an amorphous, abstract process that involves imagination and right-brained, nonlinear thinking. They look for the big picture and are interested in relationships, possibilities, and meanings. The formula $E = MC^2$ was, so the story goes, discovered by Albert Einstein in his sleep. He then set about deriving the proof. Listening or contemplative prayer is an intuitive activity.

Jung's third vector is the thinking-feeling continuum. Thinkers are ducks-in-a-row persons who prefer logical reasoning and are skeptical, impersonal, and truthful. If possible, they will stand outside a situation to observe and analyze the cause and effect. Theologians are thinkers.

Persons on the feeling end of the coninuum make decisions by valuing the alternatives. They apply personal priorities to choose what feels good or right over what feels bad or wrong. Their decisions tend to be more weighted toward the emotional, rather than derived through cognitive processes. They are often trusting and persuasive. Social activists tend to be feeling persons.

The fourth vector is the judging-perceiving continuum. Such persons tend to be judging, and like their lives ordered, structured, and planned. They usually make decisions easily without the requirement of a lot of data. They know what they want and who they like. And they like to be right. Administrators usually tend to be judging types.

Persons on the perceiving end of the continuum tend to react to the environment and to be flexible, adaptable, and tolerant, rather than take responsibility for ordering the world around them. They usually see many, even too many, sides to a question and may have a difficult time coming to a decision. They have the capacity to respond to situations in a variety of ways. Hopefully, psychotherapists and pastoral counselors tend to be perceptives.

Jung believed that the process of becoming whole meant that adult development should be such as to bring the individual to the center of each continuum, although in most cases this does not happen. To remain at either pole meant that one had less freedom and fewer choices of behavior. To be too far toward the judging pole, for instance, meant that one made premature decisions without adequate data, such as snap assessments of another's character. On the other hand, to be too far toward the perception pole might mean that one simply could not make decisions at all, because one could not see the forest for the trees.

Interestingly enough, research has demonstrated that the typical clergyperson is an ENFJ, or an Extroverted, iNtuitive, Feeling, Judger. This type suits a profession that requires a love of being with people large amounts of the time, as well as public speaking (E). Religious professionals also must have a nose for what is going on in a relationship and be able to extract meaning from events (N). They usually are concerned with values (F), and most often their job requires them to be administrators (J). Of course there are other types in the clergy as well, most notable the INFJs (Introverted, iNtuitive, Feeling, Judger), who tend to be mystics, as well as ENTJs (Extroverted, iNtuitive, Thinking, Judger), who tend to be visionaries and theologians.

Personality Type and the Pitfalls of Pastoring

Unfortunately, the very traits that make good religious professionals also can lead to sexual acting out. It seems that 70 percent of clergy, both male and female, are at the feeling end of the continuum. According to Roy Oswald and Otto Kroeger of the Alban Institute,[7] these types are more likely to get caught up in others' lives than thinking types, who can usually quite clearly see the logical consequences of sexual acting out. "Feelers" may be impulsive and blind to long-term consequences. To further compound the problem, the "F" factor also tends to make Feelers warm, loving, caring, and easy to fall in love with, particularly for a congregant who is experiencing an empty or abusive home life.

Oswald and Kroeger also believe that NF (iNtuitive, Feeling) types are the most seductive of all four temperaments, as they seem to easily seduce themselves into believing that sexual activity is what is best for the congregant. With respect to types other than ENFJ, the ENFPs (Extroverted, iNtuitive, Feeling, Perceptive) and ESFPs (Extroverted, Sensitive, Feeling, Perceptive), according to these researchers, may have a tendency to escalate a relationship with someone they find attractive. The "P" preference lends a desire to be open to the spontaneity of the moment, while the "F" preference may cause them to be touchy-feely and romantic. These researchers find the NF of the ENFP the most romantic and idealistic of all the types and the least concerned with the practical consequence of sexual involvement. Oswald and Kroeger also find that the SP of the ESFP lends vulnerability toward being drawn into the action of the moment, making it difficult to keep flirtatious behavior within appropriate boundaries. The preference for extraversion exacerbates the situation because the types are energized by others. It is important for clergy with the "E" type to have "F" values that are strong and steady with regard to noninvolvement, so that they be able to withstand temptation towards inappropriate sexual acting out.

The State of the Union

While the personality traits measured by the Myers-Briggs type indicator are fairly stable over time, or at least shift only very gradually with maturation, personality *states* are transitory, environmentally dependent, and readily impacted by learning, which is why psychotherapy works and why spiritual development is possible. One of the most interesting indicators of psychological state is the well-researched and validated Personal Orientation Inventory[8]

(POI) developed by Everett Shostrom, which uses the self-actualization theory of Abraham Maslow, one of the fathers of humanistic psychology. Instead of measuring pathology, as does the commonly used MMPI or Minnesota Multiphasic Personality Inventory, the POI is an indicator of positive mental health and the achievement of adult development, or *self-actualization.*

The POI has not been extensively used for groups limited to clergy, and little has been done with this group in the last ten years. However, four studies in the 1970s and 1980s are interesting. In 1970,[9] a large-scale study of the American Catholic Priesthood was completed, followed by one in 1979 of Catholic priests and bishops, and another in 1972 of clergymen entering a clinical training program. Finally, a study of clergy couples was done in 1988.

In the 1970 study it was found that priests who had higher actualizing scores on the POI also perceived a conflict between the current and the ideal distribution of institutional power. They felt a need to reform the church with respect to the exercise of personal initiative, and they were unhappy with the birth control encyclical. The relatively more self-actualizing priests also tended to hold less traditional values and were less apt to remain in the priesthood.

The 1979 study reported an overall profile from just slightly below to level with the norm for adults, with these Roman clergy scoring lowest on scales that measured one's sensitivity to one's own needs and feelings, and one's ability to be accepting of feelings of anger and aggression expressed by another. These priests scored highest on scales that measured one's felt sense of self-worth, one's capacity to be accepting of self in spite of weaknesses, and a third scale that measured the degree to which one sees humanity as essentially good.

The 1972 study of clergy clinical-training candidates indicated that these clergy also scored about the same as the normal adult sample, with some exceptions. They scored somewhat lower on scales that measured one's tendency to hold values that are similar to self-actualizing people, one's ability to be flexible in the application of values, and again, one's ability to be accepting of feelings of anger and aggression expressed by another.

In 1988 a study[10] was done of clergy couples, most of whom had had significant prior therapy experience. The couples were pretested, then engaged in group family of origin work,[11] and finally posttested. While achieving a profile near or above the norm for adults, these couples scored lowest on scales that measured their flexibility in the application of values, their ability to be accepting of their selves in spite of weaknesses, their tendency to see humanity as essentially good, and their capacity to have warm, interpersonal relationships. They scored highest on scales that measured their tendency to hold self-actualizing values, their sensitivity to their own needs and feelings, their ability to freely express their feelings behaviorally, their ability to see opposites of life as meaningfully related, and their ability to be accepting of feelings of anger and aggression from another. After the family of origin work, and upon retesting, these couples demonstrated significant increases in their ability to be sensitive to their own needs and feelings, and their tendency to see humanity as essentially good.

Overall, this information indicates that at least for the samples tested, clergy as a group seem to have a level of adult development that generally follows the normal profile for adults, although Catholic priests who were somewhat to very dissatisfied with the priesthood seemed to score higher self-actualizing values. Not surprisingly, for people that generally want to be liked, two of the clergy samples tested indicated some minor difficulty tolerating the expression of anger and aggression by others. Clergy in the 1988 experiment also demonstrated that with a little work the best can get better, particularly with respect to their sensitivity to their own needs and feelings as well as their outlook on the goodness of man, which is necessary to the development of trusting and intimate relationships.

Finally, one of the most interesting findings of the 1988 study of clergy couples was that these clergy all tended to be what Shostrum called *pseudoactualized:* that is, the participants knew where they wanted to be behaviorally, but they had not yet achieved this goal. As psychotherapists we are aware that cognitive understanding usually precedes behavioral change by a large margin. This is because change does not occur until there is a cognitive-emotional synthesis, an "Ah ha" experience in which an emotional, early-childhood, survival decision has been let go so that the new cognitive learning can operate. A similar process of cognitive-emotional synthesis occurs in spiritual-conversion experiences, near-death experiences being perhaps a more common subset of these. In conversion experiences, however, the event so powerfully upsets the subject's equilibrium as to enable both the cognitive and the emotional learning to occur at the same time. Pseudoactualization is the first part of what might be called a "delayed-conversion experience." This phenomenon is also probably quite common in the pulpit, where preachers often exhort us to high principles but find these same standards difficult to live out in their daily lives.

SUMMARY

Most of us have a tendency to idolize our leaders and turn them into gods by transferring onto them our own internalized image of the good object. When we see our clergyleaders as the perfect parents we never had, we are willing to overlook even their gross misbehaviors in order to maintain our very dearly held illusion.

Clergy, however, may have webbed feet instead of golden crowns, and like the rest of us, are a product of their biology and their history. They frequently come from dysfunctional families and may have inherited any number of damaging tacit family rules or behavioral scripts that diminish their self-esteem and impair their functioning in relationships.

Clergy are drawn to ministry partially because their personalities are suited to it. The ENFJ typology is particularly tailored to the task of pastoring a congregation. However, the same and similar typologies may make clergy vulnerable to inappropriate, sexual acting out. Although for the most part they are as mature or self-actualized as the general population, clergy often find it difficult to practice what they preach.

Chapter 4

Mirroring God: Clergy in Relationship

As the Reverend Rachel Hosmer, OSH, so beautifully put it, in her book *Gender and God: Love and Desire in Christian Spirituality,*[1] we mirror God, not as individuals, but in relationship. And this relationship is always a work in progress. The image of who we are is only seen and developed in the presence of the other. Two great Gestalt therapists, Erving and Miriam Polster, have said it well, "I am alone, yet to live I must meet you."[2] It is not in solitude, but in the interaction with another that we test out our beliefs about ourselves and risk relationships.

Clergypersons, of course, are not gods but very *human* beings, albeit intelligent and for the most part well-studied ones. As a result of their biology and their history, particularly with respect to early-childhood experience, they image God imperfectly, as we all do. Frequently clergy have difficulties in their family of procreation[3] partnerships as well as in their congregational partnerships. They choose their profession for a variety of reasons, and both marital and congregational relationships become the true test of their spiritual vocation. Because clergy often come from dysfunctional families, they are frequently referred to as "wounded healers." Unfortunately, in a small portion of cases, they remain too wounded and can do more damage than healing.

RELATIONSHIP AS MARRIAGE

One of the most demanding relationships that we can enter into is marriage. It is hard to maintain a facade when one is face to face with another on a daily basis. As a result, marriage is one of the most powerful tools that exists for personal development, individuation, or self-actualization. It is also a powerful instrument for self-destruction when entered without awareness and with a great deal of emotional baggage from one's family of origin.

Marriage is one of the primary places where we are challenged to become conscious of our strengths and weaknesses and grow into wholeness by finishing our "old business." It is here that we are daily challenged to fill in the empty spaces left by the trials of our youth. The psychotherapist Harville Hendrix writes about this process well in his book titled, *Getting the Love You Want: A Guide for Couples.* He also says, quite poignantly, "Marriage is a psychological and spiritual journey that begins in the ecstasy of attraction, meanders through a rocky stretch of self-discovery, and culminates in the creation of an intimate, joyful, lifelong union."[4] That is when marriage is at its best.

Marriage is hard work. It requires two to till the soil and fertilize it, if it is to have a chance at flowering. Clergy are at a considerable disadvantage in this struggle because married clergy are often expected to model this relationship perfectly, while being closely observed. I doubt many of us would like that task. In addition, clergy may enter this challenging relationship at a considerable disadvantage.

When clergy enter professional life with a sense of low self-esteem, similar to nurses, teachers, and mental health professionals, they intuitively hope to enable themselves to feel more worthwhile by being of service to others. In this attempt, some clergy overwork themselves to the detriment of their health and marriages. When a clergy marriage is in trouble, it leaves the individual much more vulnerable to inappropriate sexual involvement, because the clergyperson is not getting the love and emotional support at home that he or she needs.

Although clergy are frequently asked to model perfection, they often may have even more difficulties with relationships than the average congregant. This hardship is compounded by the reality that life in the parsonage is often very public. Clergy, by nature of their positions as symbolic exemplars, live in a fishbowl with everyone watching. Trying to live the perfect life is more than taxing.

One of the results of this stress is that divorce is increasingly common. Although divorce has historically been allowed in the Jewish religion, divorce among Protestant Christian clergy prior to thirty years ago was a rare phenomenon. For Protestants, the decision to divorce severely jeopardized the professional role because Christianity has traditionally eschewed divorce, and congregations and judica-tories (national and regional denominational administrations) were unwilling to *call* or employ divorced persons.

In the United States, however, the attitude toward divorce and the stigma attached to it began to change in the late 1960s and early 1970s. Most states have now promulgated a no-fault divorce law, so that proof of the commission of grievous acts such as adultery or abuse by one party is no longer required in order to terminate the marriage. In addition, a marital contract may be dissolved at the will of either party, even over the objection of the other partner. This, needless to say, has made divorce much easier.

Divorce amongst Protestant Christian clergy has been strongly affected by this shift. In a report of the American Episcopal Church,[5] the rate of clergy divorce from 1980 to 1983 may have approached or even exceeded 7.62 per thousand clergy per year. This may be compared to a national divorce rate of 4.9 divorces per thousand population per year as reported by the U.S. Census of 1985. There were strong indications from an additional in-depth study done in the Episcopal Diocese of Florida[6] that many more clergy, though not divorced, had serious problems in their churches and their marriages.

In an earlier study[7] involving the participation of 56 out of 60 presbyteries of the Presbyterian Church in the United States, it was reported for Presbyterian clergy that in contrast to the general popula-tion the most common clergy divorce was not among the young nor the recently married. In fact, the median age of the divorced clergy was 43.5 years, with marriages that lasted 14.5 years. Only 17 percent of the terminated marriages in the study were less than five years duration and 22 percent lasted twenty-one years or longer. The average length of the ministries of the divorcing clergy was 17.3 years prior to divorce. This study also discovered that the typical divorcing clergy was one of an emerging population. It found that almost half (46 percent) of the ever-divorced ministers in the sample had been divorced just two years prior to the 1980 study, and three-fourths had been divorced in the prior five years. The age of these divorcing clergy may be an indication of a bulge, however, at a time when divorce amongst the ordained was becoming acceptable.

This perception seems to be confirmed by the latest Hartford Seminary study (1995)[8] which indicates that, of a 1993/1994 sample of 4,500 clergy in fifteen denominations, 25 percent of clergywomen and 20 percent of clergymen are ever-divorced. This compares to a current divorce rate of 23 percent of women and 22 percent of men, as cited by the same 1985 U.S. Census.

The divorce rate, however, is far higher in the liberal denominations than in the more conservative ones. One example cited in the Hartford Seminary study was that nearly half of the Unitarian clergywomen and only slightly fewer men have been divorced, as have over a fourth of the Episcopalian clergywomen and men. In contrast, no more than a sixth of the Southern Baptist and Brethren clergywomen and men reported ever being divorced. It is also interesting to note that of the total ever-divorced clergy sample, 45 percent of women and 19 percent of men were divorced before seminary, 20 percent of women and 13 percent of men divorced during seminary, and 35 percent of women and 68 percent of men divorced after ordination.

An increasing body of literature[9] has been written on clergy divorce and the stresses on clergy marriage. Often clergy have difficulty seeking outside assistance, delaying until it is too late to save the relationship. In addition to family of origin "old baggage," many issues have been cited as contributing to the stresses on clergy marriage. These issues include the unclear role of the modern-day clergyperson in an increasingly sectarian society; the unrealistic expectations clergypersons have of themselves regarding productivity and perfection in their personal and family lives; congregational expectations of the contributions of the clergyspouse; high visibility and lack of privacy; lack of practical training in seminary to meet the problems inherent in congregational life; and even the impact of seminary training itself, as an agent that promotes rapid and unbalanced personal growth of seminarians in relation to their spouses.

RELATIONSHIP AS VOCATION

As we have discussed earlier, the clergyperson's relationship with his or her congregation may also be similar to a marriage. This contract is also a force for growth and awareness—or destruction—of both the clergyperson and the congregation. Clergy are "called" to their vocation for both the right and the wrong reasons. Relationship is the "refining fire" that tests their metal.

The Meaning of Vocation

A vocation is more than a job. It is an activity in which the meaning value and the passion of one's involvement exceeds the value of the financial compensation. Certainly this is true of ministry, which for the most part provides meager, and sometimes no monetary reward although it requires extensive and expensive education. Clergy have a sense that they are called by God to God's service. The more introverted personality types may feel driven to serve by an unexplainable numinous force, the *Hound of Heaven*, that will not let them alone otherwise. The more extroverted types may simply feel happy, comfortable, and at home in the role. The *call*, however, is a bit more complicated than it would seem.

The Process of Discernment

Listening to God is a delicate and sometimes arduous process. Because God no longer writes out his or her will on stone tablets, the determination of what that will is must be made through a process of spiritual discernment. In time-honored fashion, this discernment has involved the authority of the religious tradition and/or scriptures, the input of the community of believers, and perhaps, in cases pertaining to individual matters, the counsel of a practiced spiritual mentor. This discernment is necessary because the needs and neuroses of the human ego are loud and legion and must be separated from the still small voice of the Holy. Discernment, however, is hardly an exact science and at best is an ongoing process.

As a result, most if not all clergy enter the profession for some of the right, and many of the wrong, reasons. Certainly a desire to serve God and one's fellow human beings is a good reason. And, if one has gifts in administration, organizational development, public speaking, social and counseling skills, keen intellectual faculties, and a love of people, ministry would seem a good fit if one were willing to sacrifice privacy and future wealth while working very hard. Unfortunately, the wrong reasons are also equally compelling.

The Swedish born Dag Hammarskjold, former Secretary of the United Nations wrote, in his posthumously published journal, *Markings*, "Pray that your loneliness may spur you into finding something to live for, great enough to die for."[10] Certainly this is a recipe for passion and for discovering an ultimately meaningful vocation. At its best, loneliness is the ability to stand firm against the tide of social opinion or the ruling majority when one believes in a particular precept, such as social justice. Moses stood on the mountain and asked God not to send him to free his enslaved people, the Israelites, from the Egyptians. Then he went and did so. Martin Luther stood before the Diet of Worms and is reported to have said in response to their demand that he recount his ninety-five theses, "This is where I stand, God help me." Martin Luther King, following in his footsteps, died because he lived for the dream of a better and more just life for African Americans. At its worst, however, loneliness is the neurotic need for affirmation, companionship, and power, born out of an empty childhood.

Vocation as a Process of Personal Growth

As God would have it, we all choose a vocation, or even a job, that will challenge us to grow through our difficult places. Some, if not all clergy carry inherited, emotional baggage into their profession, including any number of dysfunctional family "messages" or rules. With hard work and goodwill, and maybe some outside help, the story can have a happy ending. Both the clergyperson and the congregation can discover themselves competent to grow in ways they had not imagined and achieve things of which they had only dreamed. They can truly become the family of God and image the holy. When the wrong reasons win out, however, we are in trouble.

The Rocks in the Road

Many clergy go into ministry at least in part because they have a need to be heard, and the pulpit provides an excellent opportunity. They may also go into ministry because having a diminished sense of self-worth, they have a need to be esteemed by others for being not only a good helper but also a holy person. They may go into ministry because they have a need to be the boss and the one in control, to assure that they are not faulted and things turn out all right. They may go into ministry because having been emotionally, physically, or sexually abused as a child, they feel powerless and have a need to exert their vested authority in order to have a sense of being powerful. They may go into ministry because being seen as holy assuages the shame and makes them feel clean.

None of these needs enhances congregational life when acted out in the context of ministry. When a spiritual leader has a need to grandstand or silence others in order to compensate for a sense of felt voicelessness, this mediates against empowering the priesthood of all believers and developing the interpretive theological gifts of congregants. A diminished self-worth may cause clergy to over-function and be a one-person show, instead of encouraging other members of the family of faith to use their time and talent to enrich the congregation. Overfunctioning also leads to resentment and clergy burnout, not to mention marital and family problems as a result of a lack of attention at home. Likewise, authoritarianism and a need for control on the part of the clergyperson also disempowers congregants, leading to apathy and a declining spiral of participation.

A need to be holy on the part of the clergyperson exacerbates the foregoing behaviors and enhances the pillar-perching stance of the symbolic exemplar. It makes being in the flesh, while living in the congregational fishbowl, fairly excruciating. Finally, a felt sense of powerlessness on the part of the clergyleader and the resultant tendency to compensate by trying to maintain a one-up position, may also set the stage for abuse, which can only occur when there is a power imbalance.

Dr. Jekyll and Mr. Hyde

Not unlike the professions of acting, politics, and university teaching, the ministry attracts persons who crave affirmation through the attention of an audience. And, not uncommonly, these persons are in such need of attention that they punish those who would take it from them. Extreme cases of such kinds of power abuse are found in persons with the Jekyll and Hyde personality, that is, persons with what mental health clinicians call narcissistic personality disorder.[11] The story of Dr. Jekyll and Mr. Hyde, written by Robert Louis Stevenson in 1886, describes a person with a dual personality, very good and very bad. The character, as depicted by Stevenson, is an applicable metaphor for the clergyperson who appears godlike, warm, and fuzzy when adored and everything is going well, and cold or rage-filled when confronted or faced with perceived competition.

Character disorders are pervasive dysfunctional formations of the personality that develop due to trauma occurring at the age of two years or earlier. From an object relations standpoint, the individual fails to integrate the good and bad object, which they may alternately transfer onto the other, sometimes in rapid succession, causing the phenomenon known as *splitting.* From the recipient's point of view, this feels as if one had been given the white cowboy hat to wear and then suddenly finding oneself wearing the black one. Because persons with character disorders often appear to be normal, gifted persons, these disorders are often difficult to identify, even by those who know the individual relatively well.

The narcissistic personality disorder is common with clergy because these individuals aggressively seek the admiration of an audience to shore up their feelings of personal inadequacy and self-hatred. They are particularly attracted to persons that put them on a pedestal, frequently have chronic feelings of envy and unsatisfied ambition, and overcompensate for their poor sense of self-esteem by a tendency toward grandiosity. Persons with this disorder usually see issues and persons in black and white terms and frequently form intense relationships that might shift suddenly from idealizing a peer, colleague, or parishioner one minute to hating him or her the next. They usually see themselves as special and have a significant sense of entitlement. Such individuals are frequently charming and proficient manipulators and have a compromised capacity for introspection and empathy. They have an intolerance of competition and criticism that causes them to scapegoat others and even appear as if they had no conscience themselves. Persons with this type of disorder project negative feelings about themselves outward onto the environment and other persons in a blaming manner.

A second character disorder also manifests itself in the clergy population. This is the sociopath or the predator. The characterological disorder, according to current clinical terminology, has been designated antisocial personality disorder. The *Fifth Draft* of the guidelines *Pastoral Misconduct: Dealing with Allegations of Sexual Contact or Harassment Within the Pastoral Relationship,* published by the Office for Church Life and Leadership of the United Church of Christ, has an adequate description:

> While appearing normal, these persons have a significant impairment and, beginning in childhood, engage in repeated antisocial and exploitive acts. Although these persons may convincingly feign remorse due to a failure of moral development, they often feel justified at having hurt, mistreated, or stolen from another. Often they are masterful at manipulating the legal or ecclesiastical system. They have no conscience and experience no guilt. Rarely have they sustained a totally monogamous relationship for more than one year, although they may appear happily married. They frequently "con" others for their own personal pleasure. They believe they are special and that the rules which apply to others do not apply to them. They often demonstrate a lack of empathy for the victim.
>
> Because persons with these disorders (including Narcissistic Personality Disorder) are often charismatic and are marvelous actors and actresses, they may effectively convince a committee on ministry they are an individual in crisis, who has only abused once and will never again abuse. (p. 13)

While persons with narcissistic personality disorder may be capable of improvement given a long term of treatment *with a therapist skilled in this specialty*, persons with antisocial personality disorder are very resistant to treatment and the prognosis for rehabilitation is poor. A person who fits this category should not be placed or continued in a position of pastoral leadership. Furthermore, it should be noted that characterological disorders often have mixed features, and persons with narcissistic personality disorder often display some of the characteristics of antisocial personality disorder.

This may seem like terrible stuff, and in reality persons with intrapsychic complications of these sorts can, and have done a great deal of damage in religious institutions—witness the Reverend Jim Jones and more recently, David Koresh. However, in working with these persons, as well as others that have hurt us, it is most wise to remember the attitude of the famous physician and hypnotherapist, Milton Erickson. Dr. Erickson believed that every person makes the best possible choice, at the time, with what he or she has available. Humanity and these individuals are not inherently bad. Instead, when children are subjected to abuse, they make what are really very creative choices in order to survive. Unfortunately, these same choices, when carried forward into adulthood without added resources, become destructive.

The Wounded Healer

During life's journey, all of us suffer from emotional wounds, and some of us sustain substantial ones. It is an anthropologically noted phenomenon that certain persons, particularly those who have suffered and managed to heal themselves of a severe and sudden illness, seem to be called to attend to the healing of others. It is as if the illness and subsequent healing was a sort of God-gifted medical school that provided the candidate with the resources to enable other persons to be restored from their infirmities. This apparently sacred wounding and subsequent recovery and vocation is termed *shamanic call* and has traditionally been associated with witchdoctors and aboriginal medicine men and women.[12] Modern-day psychotherapists and clergypersons[13] have often been depicted as wounded healers or modern shamans.

To the extent that we confront our wounded selves and take responsibility for our own healing, we do develop the resources to aid other sufferers along the path. The good news about family-of-origin dysfunction is that we are given plenty of material to experiment with, a knowledge of the pain that can be produced, an opportunity to develop empathy for others, and the possibility of a meaningful vocation. The choice then becomes ours.

SUMMARY

God is mirrored in relationship, and clergy, as the rest of us, mirror God imperfectly. Marriage is one of our most challenging relationships. It can be the most rewarding, or it can be the most destructive. Married clergy are often expected to model this relationship perfectly, while being closely observed, even though they often begin this journey at a considerable disadvantage. The marital success of clergy, as measured by current divorce rates, is about the same as that of the nonclergy population as a whole. When clergy marriages begin to fail, clergy become vulnerable to extramarital attractions as they search to get their needs for love and emotional support met.

Persons choose ministerial vocations for some of the right and some of the wrong reasons. Often clergy hope to get from the congregation some of the same things they attempt in their marriages, such as a sense of control, the ability to be heard, and a feeling of self-worth. This may work to disempower the congregation, to the disadvantage of both, or even set the stage for abuse.

In addition, ministry attracts persons who crave affirmation through the attention of an audience and/or have a desire for power. As a result, a percentage of persons with severe character or personality disorders are finding themselves among the ordained. Even though they may be charismatic and otherwise talented, persons with Narcissistic and Antisocial Personality Disorders are manipulative, self-serving, and destructive and are not fit for the job of ministry.

Finally, many if not most clergy fit the profile of the wounded healer. As such, their own difficulties and psychic injuries may be the resource from which they learn to not only heal themselves but enable the healing of the people of God.

Chapter 5

The Issue of Clergy Sexual Misconduct

This chapter has been included because while clergy sexual misconduct is often alluded to in the literature, what it actually is, and the mechanisms of how it happens are rarely explained. This has the interesting effect of keeping the matter functionally a secret, known only to the privy few—the perpetrators, the victims, and the professionals.

The sexual misconduct of spiritual leaders is not confined to any one denomination or religious faith. North American Christians, Jews, Buddhists, Sufis, and Hindus have all experienced boundary violations of this sort in their families of faith. Partially this is the result of personal psychology combined with authoritarian forms of social structuring. Partially this is the result of stirring up the right side of the brain, which is cohabited by both the activities of sex and prayer—an ancient awareness and ancient struggle of all who have pursued celibate mystical paths. Always, however, sexual misconduct is a rupture of the covenant of trust between clergyperson and congregant.

SEXUAL HARASSMENT AND SEXUAL ABUSE

It is perhaps shocking to say that sexual abuse and harassment are so commonplace in human society that up until recently they have been for the most part invisible. Like the proverbial elephant in the living room that one must walk around but cannot see, demeaning jokes about women and gay persons are such common practices in American culture, that they go unnoticed or seem acceptable. Similarly, it is generally assumed that equally qualified women should earn less compensation than men in the workplace for similar task loads. Likewise, the so-called "double standard" still persists that expects "good" women to be sexually abstinent, somewhat like the Virgin Mary, while "manly" men are assumed to be sexually promiscuous.

Sexual harassment is probably less well understood than sexual abuse. Both imply a victim and a victimizer. Sexual harassment contains the intent or threat inherent in inappropriate sexual activity, without the explicit act, and creates an environment that is anxiety-producing, offensive, or hostile. Sexual abuse is an overt action of an inappropriately sexual nature perpetrated by a person of superior position, status, age, or physical power upon another.

Many religious denominations have developed guidelines for defining sexual abuse and harassment, as well as profiles of perpetrator types and suggestions for dealing with the matter. Some, particularly those that have centralized polities with power at the top, have legislated such things as mandatory clergy background checks, and mandatory awareness training in this area for clergy and lay leaders. Less centralized denominations are not capable of legislating action for constituent regional judicatories or local congregations, and are therefore more vulnerable to persistent problems.

Sexual Harassment

The varied aspects of the concept of sexual harassment are well described in the *Fifth Draft* of the *Manual on Pastoral Misconduct* developed by the Office for Church Life and Leadership of the United Church of Christ.[1] Accordingly, sexual harassment may be defined as:

> Sexual advances, requests for sexual favors, and/or other verbal or physical conduct of a sexual nature when:
>
> a. submission to such is made either explicitly or implicitly a term of an individual's employment or their continued status in an institution; or
> b. submission to or rejection of such conduct by an individual is used as a basis for employment decisions affecting such individuals; or
> c. such conduct has the purpose or effect of interfering with work performance by creating an intimidating, hostile, or

offensive work environment based on the declared judgment of the affected individual; or

d. such conditions create an intimidating, hostile, or offensive environment for another individual regardless of the
specific setting or circumstances or the relationship between the two individuals most directly involved.

An example of instance (a) could be a situation in which the
office manager, on repeated occasions and with increasing insis-
tence, asks one of his supervisees out for a date. The manager might
be up-front about the fact that the employee's promotion depends
upon acceptance of the request, or the manager might only imply
the tenuousness of the employee's circumstance through looks, tone
of voice, and body language. A similar example could also be the
Warden of the Vestry who received the subtle message that reelec-
tion depended upon his or her compliance with the sexually inappropriate wishes of the senior pastor.

An example of instance (b) could be a situation in which a young
model or star was given a job or a part depending upon whether or
not he or she was willing to sleep with the casting director. This
would also be similar to the church secretary who was given a poor
performance review by the senior pastor because he or she was not
open to his or her advances, and as a result, was not given a raise.

An example of instance (c) would be a situation where an employee, or person in an inferior, hierarchical position was given an
undue proportion of odorous or dangerous tasks, or was subjected
to constant severe criticism and other forms of punishment as a
result of the individual's decision not to comply with or accept
sexually offensive verbal or physical behavior. This could also be
the junior clergyperson who became exhausted because he or she
was delegated all the youth work, six evening meetings a week, and
little or no opportunity to preach as a result of noncompliance to the
sexually inappropriate demands of the senior minister. It could also
be the just-graduated seminarian who lived in fear that he or she
would not be ordained because of his or her decision not to accede
to the inappropriate sexual requests of a member of the pastoral
staff. Pointed homophobic comments by a senior pastoral staff

member to a gay junior staff member would also be included under this rubric.

Finally, situation (d) addresses secondary victims of sexual harassment. These are persons who are affected by the consequences of the sexual harassment, although they themselves were not the primary target. An example of this instance would be the secretary who was told by his or her manager that something bad would happen to him or her if he or she divulged the secret regarding the affair the department head was having with another employee. A similar circumstance would be one in which the junior pastor was warned by the senior pastor that he or she would be fired and his or her career ruined if he or she divulged the secret of the affair that the senior pastor was having with a parishioner.

Sexual Abuse

Like sexual harassment, sexual abuse always implies a power differential between the abused and the abuser, the victim and the victimizer. Sexual abuse includes the following:

1. Sexual contact with a minor. This may be in the form of fondling of the breasts, buttocks, or genitals; undressing, exposure, or peeping; vaginal or rectal penetration, fellatio, or cunnilingus (oral contact with the genitals); inappropriately sexualized hugs and kisses; or suggestive comments. This list is not exhaustive. A generally useful guideline for gray areas such as hugs is whether or not the minor feels generally uncomfortable and/or threatened, and it can be determined that the hugs, in this case, were excessive or unwarranted.
2. Rape or physical sexual contact with the breasts, buttocks, or genitals of any adult using force, threat, or intimidation. Marital rape is also sexual abuse.
3. Sexual malfeasance. Malfeasance is the performance by a public official (or clergyperson) of an act that is legally unjustified, harmful, or contrary to law or *an act in violation of public trust*. In this situation, sexual malfeasance is the breach of trust that occurs between a clergyperson and a congregant within the ministerial or professional relationship as a result of sexual contact with the breasts, buttocks, or pubic area. [2] (This does

not include respectful relationships between spouses.) It can also include behaviors such as indecent exposure. Initially the recipient may be accepting, either as a result of what can be called *transference love* or from a desire to please the pastor or professional while trusting that the professional is acting in the recipient's best interest. Since, in the case of a clergyperson, the professional, has by nature of his or her position been entrusted with the recipient's (or in this case victim's) soul, in the best of cases, and for the most functional congregants, this is not a great leap of faith. Congregants do not expect their clergyperson to abuse them, and, like the woman who comes to premarital counseling and observes the priest masturbating under his desk during the interview—they are confused and confounded by such behavior. Usually they try to ignore it, and certainly they don't talk about it. The concepts of a breach of trust and transference love will be covered further later in this chapter.

4. Offensive, sexualized, behaviors. This includes body language such as sexualized winks and leers; physical contact such as pinching, tickling, or touching without permission that has felt sexual overtones for the receiver; unwarranted hugs or kisses, particularly full-body hugs and French kisses; and suggestive or crude language.

THE ISSUE OF POWER: ABANDONMENT, AUTHORITY, AND ANIMAL FORCE

In Chapter 1 we began to touch upon the issue of power. Here it is important to reiterate that advantage is a powerful determinant in relationships. And it is also worth repeating that human beings do not cause displeasure to those whom they perceive as more power-ful. Such an action simply does not have survival value. To the extent that we are able and willing to risk rejection and reprisal, we have discovered a power within us that exceeds that derived from position, status, or economic advantage. Some would call the abil-ity, capacity, or state of mind *the peace of God*. The saints and martyrs found it, and some of us at various times in our lives, though rarely consistently, find it also. Most of the time, however, we acknowledge that there are persons more powerful than ourselves. The *power of abandonment,* the *power of authority,* and *animal force* are the forms of power that most often enter into the equation of clergy sexual misconduct.

The Power of Abandonment

From a spiritual/psychological standpoint, most of the time when we acknowledge the superior power of another, we have actually traded our own power, given it away in exchange for something that we believe is more valuable. Most often the commodity that we are after is a sense of security or at least the illusion of security. A woman, for instance, believes, albeit sometimes at an unconscious level, that she should not stand up to her husband's disrespectful behavior or self-serving wishes because to do so might risk his leaving and therefore a loss of required financial support. In this way she gives away her power and her personhood in exchange for a sense of economic stability. As we have seen from the criteria for abuse and harassment listed above, coercion based upon the threat of losing one's job, or job opportunity, is also a power move that plays upon the victim's reasonable desire for economic/vocational well-being, as well as his or her illusion of security.

We also give away our power in order to garner affirmation and a sense of being special, cared for, or loved. Since clergy are for the most part held up as special persons, even to the extent of being equated with God or beloved parent/good object, affirmation and special attention from these persons is often particularly prized. For a hungry, empty individual that special attention is hard to turn down, even when it is inappropriately sexualized. Both of these situations, economic and emotional, illustrate what might be called the power of abandonment.

The Power of Authority

Of course, particularly in the case of children, the raw *power of authority,* similar again to the authority of God or a parent, comes into play. Children raised in households where the rule is "theirs not to make reply, theirs not to reason why, theirs but to do and die,"[3] are easily coerced into participating in uncomfortable behaviors. Adults that are raised in authoritarian households are also susceptible to this form of power, particularly if they have been abused. In this case, the capacity to say "no" is often attenuated. We will cover more about this later. Finally, doing the will of God may become confused with doing the will of the clergyperson, in whom ultimate trust is often placed.

Animal Force

Last, of course, there is the power of brute, animal force or the threat of physical death or injury, as in the case of rape. Since, as organisms, humans are programmed to survive, victims often submit for fear of even worse consequences should they resist. Force is then usually combined with some form of coercion in which victims are prodded to give away their spiritual/psychological power by keeping the secret, even if only out of shame or the fear that no one will believe them.

HOW IT HAPPENS: MISCONDUCT FROM THE PART OF THE PERPETRATOR

As we have discussed, all sexual misconduct occurs because a power differential exists between the perpetrator and victim, whether or not the situation is one of harassment or one of outright abuse. This power imbalance may be one of status, vested authority, hierarchy, age, gender, or physical strength. In general, perpetrators have themselves been victims and are generally confused about what love really is. They may have learned in their families of origin the rule, "Love means being hurt or used." As we saw in Chapter 3 this may also be translated, "If you want my love, affection, attention, you have to give me your body," and "If you don't let me use your body, you don't love me."

Perpetrators may be divided into five broad, although not discontinuous, sections: pedophiles, persons with other paraphilias, sexual addicts, predators, and situational abusers. Each has a particular modus operandi and a psychology that drives their behavior. While we will not undertake an exhaustive explanation here, hopefully what follows will lend some clarity to the differences between the several types of abusers and their relative capacities for rehabilitation.

The Pedophile

The pedophile is a person that is often developmentally emotionally arrested and has difficulties forming satisfying intimate emotional relationships with adults. These individuals are frequently able to feel competent and powerful only in the company of youngsters. By definition,[4] the focus of sexual activity of these persons is with prepubescent children, generally thirteen years or younger. Some of these individuals prefer girls, some boys, and some are aroused by both males and females. Some pedophiles may also be attracted to adults.

Persons with this disorder may limit their activity to exposing themselves, undressing the child and looking, masturbating in the presence of the child, or gentle touching and fondling of the child. Others may perform fellatio or cunnilingus on the child or penetrate the child's vagina or anus with fingers, foreign objects, or a penis.

The perpetrator may rationalize these actions by saying that they have "educational value" for the child—that the child enjoys this sort of attention and even derives sexual pleasure from it. Perpetrators may also excuse their behavior by saying that the child was "sexually provocative." These individuals may lure the child into the situation by being attentive to the child's needs to gain his or her affection and loyalty and thereby prevent the child from telling the secret.

Pedophiles may limit their sexual involvement to children, stepchildren, and relatives (incest), or they may victimize children outside the family as well. In these cases, they typically gain access by becoming involved in organizations such as Girl Scouts or Boy Scouts or by taking jobs as camp counselors, gym teachers, coaches, nursery school attendants, youth ministers, or the like. The course of this disorder is chronic, and the tendency of these individuals to return to pedophilic behavior, even after treatment, is high. Recidivism is twice as high in persons preferring males as it is for those who prefer females.

Persons with Other Paraphilias

Paraphilias are medically defined as recurrent, intense sexually arousing fantasies, sexual urges, or behaviors generally involving (1) nonhuman objects, (2) the suffering or humiliation of oneself or one's partner, or (3) children or other nonconsenting persons, that occur over a period of at least six months.[5] Pedophilia, described above, is one of the paraphilias. Other paraphilias include: *fetishism*, the use of a nonliving object for sexual arousal; *frotteurism*, sexual arousal achieved from touching or rubbing against a nonconsenting person; *exhibitionism*, sexually arousing fantasies and behaviors involving the exposure of one's genitals to an unsuspecting person; *voyeurism*, behaviors engaged in for the purpose of sexual arousal involving the act of observing unsuspecting individuals, usually strangers, who are naked or who are in the process of disrobing or engaging in sexual intercourse; *sexual masochism,* the need to be beaten, bound, humiliated, or otherwise made to suffer in order to achieve sexual arousal; and *sexual sadism*, which involves the commission of real, not imagined acts, of psychological or physical suffering upon the victim from which the perpetrator derives sexual excitement. While fetishism and sexual masochism are rarely the causes of clergy sexual misconduct, because they do not require a nonconsenting victim, the other paraphilias—frotteurism, exhibitionism, voyeurism, and sexual sadism—do require a victim and as such represent a dangerous distortion in psychosexual development.[6]

Sexual Addicts

Sexual addiction is a compulsive behavior similar to gambling. It may be defined as an obsessional and emotional attachment to sexual fantasies and behavior that have a pervasive negative impact on the person's life[7] (and perhaps the lives of other persons). Persons affected with this disorder have a need for constant sexual stimulation and a history of traumatic early experiences, especially childhood sexual abuse. As with other compulsive disorders, this may be an anxiety containment or stress-relief attempt to fill the mind with thoughts of an activity, or the activity itself, in order to avoid having room for more anxiety provoking reflections. It may also be the result of an insatiable emptiness and need to be held. The diagnostic signs of addiction are:

1. Preoccupation and obsession with thoughts and fantasies related to the activity.
2. Experienced by the individual as a drive-based craving and need.
3. A sequence of patterned, ritualistic, goal-directed behavior aimed at satisfying the perceived need.
4. Psychological dependence on the feelings and moods associated with the behavior, especially in times of stress.
5. The presence of conscious and unconscious defense processes that attempt to maintain the addiction.
6. An increased tolerance and a tendency for the problem to increase in severity as more frequent repetition is needed in order to obtain the same level of satisfaction or relief from tension.
7. Withdrawal symptoms that include restlessness, agitation, and irritability when there is a barrier to engaging in the behavior.
8. An increasing loss of ability to control the frequency, duration, and circumstances under which the behavior occurs, along with a coexisting desire to reduce or eliminate the behavior.
9. The presence of a variety of unwanted consequences that create serious social, family, health, financial, and legal problems, including divorce, job loss, and incarceration.[8]

The Predator

Sexual sadists and many pedophiles are certainly predators. However, for purposes of this typography, we will consider predators as persons who more often abuse adult, and do so without the explicit intention of deriving sexual excitement by inflicting pain and upon the victim. The victim may be same sex or opposite sex.

Rather, the predator is a person who derives a sense of power and status through the sexual misuse of other individuals. He or she will also have a tendency to see other persons as objects, toys, or *things* to be acquired or used, rather than human beings with souls and feelings. This sort of person will also be generally confused about what love really is. A good example of the behavioral psychology of the predator is found in Arthur Miller's classic play, *Death of a Salesman*. Here, Willie Loman's son, a salesman like his father, is found to be a womanizer who compensates for his felt-sense of powerlessness by "ruining" young women. Of his habit, Happy and his brother, Biff, say the following:

> *Happy:* I gotta show some of those pompous, self-important executives over there that Hap Loman can make the grade. I want to walk into the store the way he walks in. Then I'll go with you, Biff. We'll be together yet, I swear. But take those two we had tonight. Now weren't they gorgeous creatures?
>
> *Biff:* Yeah, yeah, most gorgeous I've had in years.
>
> *Happy:* I get that any time I want, Biff. Whenever I feel disgusted. The only trouble is, it gets like bowling or something. I just keep knockin' them over and it doesn't mean anything. You still run around a lot?
>
> (From *Death of a Salesman* by Arthur Miller. Copyright 1949, renewed ©1977 by Arthur Miller. Used by permission of Viking Penguin, a division of Penguin Books USA Inc.)

In particular, as it turns out, Happy makes a habit of bolstering his diminished sense of self-esteem by seducing the financées of the company executives, just prior to the couples' weddings. For Happy, sexual exploitation is a way of becoming bigger and getting even.

Predators may also be personality disordered, particularly of the narcissistic or antisocial type mentioned in Chapter 4.[9] Persons with either of these disorders are extremely self-serving. The narcissistic type seduces the victim with his (more often than her) charming, warm, fuzzy side because he enjoys the attention and audience, which bolsters self-esteem while filling a deep felt sense of emptiness and loneliness. Narcissistic persons are usually very good at "selling" themselves. In addition, the grandiosity, which is consistent with this disorder, enables this sort of individual to believe either that sexual favors are his due or that the victim is actually pursuing the predator.

The antisocial type seduces or simply abuses the victim because he or she finds it titillating. Since these persons have poor super-ego development, it gives them a power rush uncountered by a sense of social conscience. Either of these types may be quite crafty in covering their tracks. They may invoke the rule of loyalty or use other forms of coercion, such as telling the victim that no one would believe that the beloved minister had done such a thing or that telling the secret would hurt the spouse, the family, or the congregation. In addition, predators are often quite intelligent, particularly clergypersons who have made it through the necessary graduate education. As such, these persons often engage in mind-bending—convincing the victim that his or her reality is not reality at all. That in fact, it is the victim who seduced the clergyperson and who is at fault.

The Situational Abuser

Finally, the situational abuser is an individual who does not habitually abuse but who may abuse when placed in stressful situations, when his or her emotional needs are not being otherwise met. This may occur during the long convalescence of a marital partner, after the loss of a child, or during a midlife crisis. This sort of abuse is most likely to occur during periods of marital difficulty of any sort, when the marital partner is emotionally unavailable. Commonly, situational abuse may be a one-time occurrence, although it does set a precedent, and should a similar situation arise again, it is often repeated.

Because clergy are fairly socially isolated by the nature of their vocation, vulnerable clergy frequently go to a congregant to get their own emotional/sexual needs met. They are often led to this "watergate" through the counseling situation, which sets up a particularly powerful transference/countertransference dynamic.

Transference/Countertransference Love

Clergy are often called upon to do counseling, whether it be for bereavement, family or personal problems, or spiritual emptiness. Unfortunately they are for the most part poorly trained for this task. Only in infrequent cases have they experienced their own therapy and/or spiritual direction so as to acquire at least an awareness of their own blind spots and vulnerabilities. When a counselee (or congregant in this case) comes to the clergyperson for help, he or she already perceives the pastor, by nature of the clerical position, to be kind, sympathetic, caring, affirming, long-suffering, strong, and godlike. This benevolent picture is called *transference* and may or may not be characteristic of the counselor in question. The clergyperson, as recipient of this rosy projection, feels competent, affirmed, and valued whether or not he or she is indeed capable of performing usefully as a counselor in an objective sense. This is called *countertransference*. Because caring and valuing are two of the most sexually arousing activities that can happen between people, this sort of transference/countertransference quickly develops into what is called *transference love*—the warm, gooey, filled-up, no-longer-lonely, safe, embraced, exhilarating, *sexually powerful* feeling that our culture has co-opted us into believing is *true love*. Every popular ballad that intones, "I feel good when I'm with you" reinforces this illusion.

The power, in fact the sheer force of the sexual attraction that arises from transference love, cannot be emphasized enough. The feelings might be compared to a tidal wave on the desert or the sight of a banquet to a starving person. Transference/countertransference love is the stuff of all infatuations and all experiences of "falling in love," which are more accurately the wishful desire to possess the fanciful "good object" that was discussed in Chapter 3. Perhaps this sounds a bit like "love's executioner,"[10] but in reality, of course, love is a multidimensional thing, a very small part of which may be "chemistry" and a very large part of which entails patience, sacrifice, and the forgiveness of ourselves as well as the other. Real love can only occur in a real relationship that has been, most often painfully, stripped of illusion so that we see one another face-to-face and not through a glass, darkly.

It is very easy for emotionally starved, overworked clergypersons to fall into the trap of believing that these powerful feelings of transference/countertransference love are signals, finally, of the love that they have never had—true love to which they now abandon themselves with little thought of the consequences. As was mentioned in Chapter 3, clergy of the ENFP and ESFP Myers-Briggs personality types are particularly prone to this sort of error, unless they have in place strong F values that mediate against clergy-congregant or counselor-congregant involvement. It is a well-known statistic that of the various persons suspended as members from the American Association of Marriage and Family Therapists every year for sexual ethical violations, clergy comprise by far the largest group.

SUMMARY

Both forms of sexual misconduct, sexual harassment and sexual abuse, imply a power differential between the victim and the victimizer. Sexual harassment contains the intent or threat inherent in inappropriate sexual activity and creates an environment that is anxiety-producing, offensive, or hostile. Sexual abuse is an overt action of inappropriately sexual nature perpetrated by a person of superior position, status, age, or physical power against another.

Advantage is an influential determinant in relationships, since human beings in their intuitive desire to survive, try not to cause displeasure to those whom they perceive as more powerful. The power of abandonment, the power of authority, and the power of physical force are the forms of power that most often enter into the equation of clergy sexual misconduct.

Perpetrators have often themselves been victims and are frequently confused about what love really is. With respect to clergy sexual misconduct, these persons may be divided into five broad, but not entirely distinct, categories: pedophiles, persons with other paraphilias, sexual addicts, predators, and situational abusers. While pedophiles and sexual addicts may be predators, the most serious predators, and often the most difficult to apprehend, are those who have personality disorders, particularly of the narcissistic or antisocial type. Situational abusers, on the other hand, are most often emotionally, needy clergy with too little training who find themselves presented with too great an opportunity. One-on-one counseling is fraught with the danger of desire created by transference/counter-transference love.

Chapter 6

Vulnerability and the Psychology of the Victim

Persons are not born victims. Instead, victims are created by the environment. In the previous chapter we discussed that aspect of the environment that has to do with the perpetrator. In the next chapter we will talk about how the wider system chooses and creates scapegoats, revictimizes, and makes new victims. Here we will look at the psychology of the victim because that which leads the individual into a sexually inappropriate relationship and keeps the person stuck there, is scantily, if ever elucidated, and it is also an important part of the picture.

We will look not only at primary victims, those who actually experience sexual abuse or harassment firsthand, but also secondary victims, those persons who get caught in and victimized by the fallout. In many cases, those persons who are aware of an incidence of sexual misconduct, although not primarily involved, are also the targets of attack, coercion, isolation, and other aggressive behaviors of the perpetrator in the service of keeping the secret. In addition, we will examine the particular vulnerability of staff, student ministers, and seminarians as both primary and secondary victims, as well as the issue of false accusation.

HOW THE PRIMARY VICTIM BECOMES INVOLVED

Victims become involved generally through one of three mechanisms: being taken by force or coercion, seduction and the unconscious lure of transference love, or an inability to say "no" to inappropriate advances because the capacity to draw that boundary has been attenuated as a result of early childhood abuse.

Force and Coercion

Being overpowered by physical strength is one of the primary ways that women and children throughout history have come to be abused. This still occurs today, not only in the genocides of the Middle East, but in places such as New York City's Central Park and in Christian and Jewish homes and families of faith. Victims find the abuse so degrading and shameful, however, that even if they are not coerced outright by the perpetrator, they often do not report the attack. In incestuous families, as well as "incestuous" families of faith, there are usually all sorts of rules in place that protect the awful secret. Rules such as "Pastor/Father/Mother can do no wrong," "Deny your experience," "Don't trust your reality because its not really real," "Its your fault," and "Be loyal" all mediate against disclosure. In families such as these, the victim rightly intuits that telling the secret can only reap reprisal.

Coercion is another form of force. Here a different form of power is used and abused—the power of position. Coercion occurs when it is hinted or overtly told to the potential victim that unless he or she cooperates, either (1) something bad will happen, (2) he or she will not get a desired position, and/or will loose his/her present position, or (3) something bad will happen to someone else. Coercion uses fear, financial leverage, and emotional blackmail. The perpetrator hopes that the fear of economic loss, or loss of status or position, or the loss of a relationship (oftentimes a preexisting one with the perpetrator), or the threat of harm to another person (often a younger sibling, or even a beloved animal), will force the victim into compliance. Perpetrators often use the "I'll die without you" ploy, suggesting that the victim is essential to the perpetrator's survival and loyalty demands accession.

Seduction and Transference Love

Oftentimes, the feelings of transference love are so overwhelming that victims really believe they are in love with the perpetrator, at least in the beginning. They may initially participate willingly. Even as they gradually grow uncomfortable about the relationship, they will continue to seek to protect their abuser rather than disclose the secret. This loyalty aspect is particularly powerful, since the victim may have experienced little care, concern, and affection elsewhere in his or her life. As a result, the individual is extremely thankful for whatever attention is received, even if this attention was merely the strategy of a planned seduction.

Furthermore, since the victim feels that he or she has gotten something from the relationship, at least initially, he or she often feels responsible for the abuse rather than the other way around. Needless to say, the perpetrator often strives to strengthen this perception. It has been an ancient myth in our culture that men are unable to control their impulses and must act-out sexually when they are aroused by, and in the vicinity of, an attractive female. Women, since Eve, have been seen to have mysterious powers that lure men, as with Odysseus's sirens, and divest them of their strength and even make them ritually unclean. (This latter is the reason that Biblically, men were not allowed to sleep with a woman before the day of battle.) In the courts, until quite recently, it was often concluded that a woman was at fault when raped because she had been flirtatious or had dressed seductively and really "wanted" to be attacked. A.W. Richard Sipe relates of the Christian Church, "If the history of the church and the calendar of saints are reviewed, virgins, martyrs, and widows are the female heroes. The sexless, the silent, and the dead are models for women."[1]

The Inability to Say "No"

The third mechanism of involvement is the real inability of victims to say "no." Perhaps this seems like a strange concept. However, when children are raised in a physically, emotionally, or sexually abusive environment, they learn that to resist is tantamount to death. Some, in fact, who do not learn this lesson soon enough, do die, or more accurately, are killed by their caretakers.

As developing beings, we typically begin our first resistances between eighteen to twenty-four months of age, usually by refusing to eat what our parents want us to eat, wear what our parents want us to wear, and do what our parents want us to do. This period has fondly been called the "terrible twos." It is a time when we establish our concept of ourselves as individuals, rather than as physical extensions of our primary caretakers. Our second major episode of resistance typically comes during the teenage years, when we refuse our parent's values, wear our hair long or in a pinkspiked mohawk, and listen to heavy metal music instead of jazz, blues, or the classical composers. Having physically separated ourselves from our parents in the two-year-old stage, we now separate our beingness—our sense of our own meaning—from that of our parents. We question, and we allow ourselves to adopt different perceptions of the world around us; we review our value system. This distancing period is frequently called the "generation gap." Finally, when we are between thirty-five and fifty years old, we will get a chance to do this again, in case we didn't get it right the first time. This stage is called "midlife crisis."

Each of these stages involves saying "no" to the perceptions and demands of our parents and the social environment around us. Saying "no" allows us to *differentiate,* to become different, unique, individual, to separate from our environment while at the same time remain connected to it. Saying "no" is the process of *drawing a boundary* between what is me, that is my feelings, thoughts, perceptions, and values, and what is you, your feelings, thoughts, perceptions, and values. In dysfunctional family systems, often a high degree of anxiety exists, usually expressed as anger, around the possibility of allowing a family member to be different. The unconscious underpinning for this anxiety is usually a fear of abandonment. That is, if you are different, we will not be hooked together and I will lose you, and if I am abandoned, I will die. Of course, this is not rational thinking for an adult, but fear and anxiety is rarely of rational origin, unless one is staring down a loaded gun barrel.

Many families do not allow their children to say "no" at the appropriate times, using either the coercion of emotional abandonment or that of physical force. Some families do not let their children say "no" to the sexual usage of their bodies by persons more powerful than themselves. Children that have been taught not to say "no" to sexual advances often become literally paralyzed, physically frozen as adults when similar advances are made by a person whom they perceive to have greater power. These "adult children," in an ancient attempt to survive, either become passive victims or pleasing participants. They play dead or seemingly willingly do whatever is asked in order not to anger or be abandoned by the abuser. Needless to say, when the abuser, through the phenomenon of transference, is Father/Mother/God, the stakes are high.

Finally, an additional difficulty inherent to growing up in an abusive household is that the child understands the abuse to be "normal." This is because the family constitutes the child's entire "world," at least until he or she goes to school, and oftentimes the school environment is itself abusive. This sense of abuse being normal, expectable, or acceptable usually persists into adulthood, resulting in a high tolerance for inappropriate and disrespectful behaviors by peers and superiors. Thus an action that would be seen as clearly abusive to a person raised in a nurturing household does not seem to be an attack, injury, or even violation to an adult child historically used to similar forms of treatment. This occurs because the victim literally does not know what a respectful relationship is or should be *since he or she has never experienced true respect.* Just as the charge to the members of the Light Brigade is, "theirs not to reply, theirs not to reason why, theirs but to do and die," the victim is charged, by authoritarian family messages in the childhood environment, not to reply to, question, or say "no" to abusive behavior and sexual advances. The victim functionally cannot give him or herself an inner permission to resist. As a result, the victim gives away his or her selfhood and dies emotionally and spiritually from compliance.

WHY THE VICTIM DOESN'T DISCLOSE

Although this subject will be touched upon in greater depth in the next chapters, it is probably important to mention here the impediments to disclosure. One might think that any sane person would be more than ready to report sexual molestation. However, this is not at all the case.[2] Victims do not disclose for one or several of four major reasons: loyalty, felt guilt, an intuition that they will not be believed, and overwhelming fear and denial.

Loyalty: The Tie That Binds

As was touched upon earlier, victims who have received little love, attention, and tenderness during their lives are very vulnerable to loyalty binds. They frequently are so appreciative of whatever affection was given them by the perpetrator that they feel a sense of significant loyalty for these small kindnesses. Furthermore, the perpetrator often makes use of this vulnerability by emphasizing to the victim that theirs is a unique and special, relationship. In these cases, the threat of the loss of the friendship or relationship is a greater cost to the victim than the abuse. When relationship versus disclosure is weighed in the balance, the relationship tips the scales, and the victim stays silent.

A variation on the loyalty theme is the victim's capacity to "understand' the abuse, which is actually an intellectual defense mechanism somewhat like denial. Examples of this might be, "He or she did it because he was lonely and had no one else to turn to, " "He or she didn't know what he or she was doing," and "He or she stopped when I told him or her to." In many ways this is a functional, survival strategy because it separates the victim from the possible feelings of guilt, anger, and anxiety, while at the same time, and even more important, it protects against feelings of powerlessness. Understanding puts the victim in the felt position of being in charge since from understanding comes choice, even if it is a fanciful one. However, because the possibility of choice may not actually be real, given the other psychological undercurrents that may deter the victim from disclosing or being able to stop the abuse, this strategy may enable the injury to continue.

Felt Guilt: The Inheritance of the Scapegoat

Felt guilt is a powerful deterrent to disclosure. This is particularly the case when the victim has been raised in a family situation where the rule is, "It is your fault." Victims keep silent because not only are they fearful of the judgment of others, but they also judge themselves harshly. In some cases, most notably with persons that have been the family scapegoat—a phenomenon we will cover in the next chapter—victims may even believe themselves to be fundamentally "bad." In reality, because the phenomenon of community scapegoating is so prominent, especially in religious systems that tend to be highly defended and often condemning of persons who break the "secrecy" rule, the specter of judgment falling heavily upon the victim is not an airy fantasy.

Not in Our House: A Failed Trust

Victims often intuit, quite rightly, that they will not be believed. Frequently, congregations overidolize their spiritual leaders and they, as with many families, can engage in considerable denial concerning the issue of the sexual misconduct of their beloved "parent." Indeed, for congregants who identify the pastor with God or their "good object," to admit that such behavior is possible is literally to lose the idyllic relationship, especially since this relationship is founded on the illusion that the spiritual leader is all light and no darkness, fully divine but not fully human. The impact of this denial on the victim is that, not only is his or her experience and reality negated, but the victim may become scapegoated in the congregation's attempt to protect and be loyal to their leader. As a result, instead of being supported in a dire time of need, the victim becomes emotionally separated, perhaps even ostracized, from his or her community, which is not only very painful but is also tantamount to spiritual death.

Spiritual death is not the only sequel, however. The pain of not being believed and the resultant isolation, added to the pain of the abuse, can be so overwhelming that it is not uncommon for victims of sexual abuse to become suicidal, even eventually taking their own lives. Suicide is a phenomenon that is poorly understood by most clinically untrained persons, including clergy. It is often dismissed as a "sin," a failure of faith, or seen as the act of an "emotionally fragile" individual. Instead, the motive for most suicides is simply the termination of intolerable pain when there seems to be no other way out. Victims can become trapped in the sexually abusive, even terroristic system, be it an incestuous family of origin or the family of faith. Unfortunately, the historic cloak of secrecy and denial regarding clergy sexual misconduct in the church has, for years, actually left no way out for victims, save voluntary excommunication with the resultant loss of emotional support systems and the loss of faith as a resource.

Overwhelming Fear and Denial

In cases where the victim has reason to fear for his or her job security or possibly even the loss of a vocation, when the victim faces certain and severe sanction as a result of cultural/religious tradition,[3] or when the victim has had a prior, perhaps unremembered history of sexual abuse, fear may become an overwhelming factor. In order to contain this anxiety, the victim may begin to deny, even to him or herself, that the incident happened. This, of course, is the beginning of the phenomenon called *repression,* the forceful forgetting of experience. When a trauma is so great that its reexperiencing is unthinkable, persons make the inner decision to bury the memory below the threshold of consciousness. In so doing, they seal off the psychic wound in much the same way the physical body walls off a tubercular abscess in the lungs. Unfortunately, although this alleviates the conscious anxiety, the psychic wound continues to fester, producing a variety of unconscious behaviors and even physical ailments. A list of symptoms of this sort, which commonly present with victims of sexual trauma, is included in the appendix.

SECONDARY VICTIMS

Secondary victims are those persons who have not directly been sexually harassed or abused but who nevertheless suffer the after-effects of the misconduct. This might include the family of the clergyperson found guilty of sexual misbehavior, who then suffers financial hardship and disgrace as a result of his or her dismissal. As will be discussed in the next chapters, secondary victims certainly include the family of the faithful who that suffer from a host of dysfunctional patterns brought about by the keeping of secrets associated with misconduct. And it includes the wider religious institution, whose followers and spiritual leaders become shrouded in shame and disrespect. But there is one more group of individuals that deserves particular attention.

Persons known to the perpetrator, who have either been witness to the abuse or who have knowledge of it, are especially vulnerable to coercive attacks by that individual, in the service of keeping the secret. In addition, should such a person disclose the abuse, they are easily scapegoated by an unbelieving congregation who out of its own anxiety and attempts at denial, tries to shoot the messenger. *While the legal system gives recourse to primary victims of sexual abuse and harassment, it does not provide any safety net, redress, or compensation for secondary victims.* This is a serious difficulty and mediates against the possibility of persons taking the risk of disclosing sexual misconduct, particularly in religious systems, a fact that has been taken ample advantage of by perpetrators.

Of this group, the persons that are at greatest risk are seminarians, student ministers, and ordained junior staff members. This is because these individuals are frequently aware of the abuse, if not directly involved,[4] and need the approval and recommendation of clergy superiors, including the perpetrator, in order to finish their ordination process, find a job, or move on to a senior position in another church. Coercion and attack by the perpetrator, in these cases, is most effective. Disclosure of sexual misconduct by a seminarian, student minister, or ordained junior staff member is well-known to be tantamount to professional suicide. Furthermore, most religious systems currently mandate that abuse must be disclosed by the primary victim in order to be prosecuted. This only encourages effective terrorism on the part of the perpetrator in order to silence both primary and secondary victims.

FALSE ACCUSATIONS

False accusations and faulty or fabricated memories of childhood sexual abuse are subjects that have gotten quite a bit of press recently. Those of us who work in the field realize that such occurrences can happen, usually as a result of poorly performed psychotherapy. However, false disclosures are relatively rare, particularly in the case of children, because disclosure has significant repercussions, including disbelief of other family members and economic and/or physical loss of removed or jailed primary caretakers. In the case of a congregant, disbelief, disenfranchisement, scapegoating, isolation, and abandonment by the family of faith are the real possibilities of bringing forward a complaint of sexual misconduct.

Although clergy often fear that angry congregants might falsely accuse them of sexual misconduct, the cost of disclosure to the plaintiff is so significant that it is never undertaken lightly or frivolously. It is not uncommon for clergy perpetrators, particularly of the predatory type, to employ the "poor me" defense, attempting to dismiss accusations as the imaginings of a congregant who had a crush or transference-love reaction upon his or her spiritual leader.[5] Certainly many individuals "fall in love" with their minister or rabbi (or psychotherapist, for that matter). However, only seriously psychologically impaired individuals would imagine that the feelings were reciprocal, unless the clergyperson confirmed that reality and then acted upon it. Of course, it is necessary to check out all the data. Nevertheless, false accusations by adult followers of a spiritual leader are so uncommon[6] that most recently, in some denominations such as the Episcopal Church,[7] the burden of proof has been placed on the defendant clergyperson.

A MATTER OF ETHICS

In closing, some authors would say that it is currently safe for primary and secondary victims to disclose their abuse, due to new awarenesses in the Church coupled with the successful resource of the criminal court system. This is actually not true in many, many cases. In large part, the real risk born by the victim has to do with the failure, to date, of many denominations—particularly decentralized denominations, as well as denominationally unaffiliated families of faith—to have established, published, ministerial codes of ethics, investigatory protocols, and adequately trained response teams, as well as victim advocates. Instead, the "old boy" system that has been so long in effect seems to function by the code of "whatever you can get away with is all right." And secrecy and denial has been and still is in many cases the norm. In short, and most simply, there is frequently no official yardstick against which to measure the conduct of a clergyperson, nor is there a defined way to go about collecting and sorting out information. Even when there are clear ethical standards in place, the victims are still often left out in the cold to fend for themselves during the process. Commonly, however, the religious body has not operationally defined offenses of sexual misconduct, nor are there endorsed, published, ethical standards through which a victim might present his or her case. In the instance of those secondary victims who are witnesses or messengers who reported abuse, their *only* redress is on ethical grounds, within the system, as the courts do not recognize injury from harassment unless the individual has been deprived of income.

Even in those denominations, such as the Orthodox and Conservative Jewish movements that are governed clearly in these cases by

Mosaic Law (Halaha) and the Jewish Reform movement, which has carefully formulated a specific code of ethics, still, in many, many cases there are no standard protocols or even resources for proceeding with an investigation, much less for disciplining an identified abuser at the local or regional level. Institutional executives and judicatory staff are gradually becoming more informed, but education of this sort is complicated and frustrated by personnel turnover. While ordained persons may be required to undertake informational training with regard to sexual harassment and abuse, frequently no such curriculum is written for or provided to the laity. In unaffiliated and free church denominations, as well as most of the Jewish movements, each regional and local judicatory, and even individual families of faith, must define and approve procedural policies, and in many cases even create ethical codes. These processes are further hampered by the degree of denial that leadership experiences with respect to these matters.

Rarely are established, published codes of ethics and procedural protocols brought into the awareness of and made available to potential victims. This is particularly true for congregants who do not hold positions of leadership. Victims are frequently not aware of the definitions of sexual harassment, the behavioral flags that signal potential abuse, or the scope of what is considered sexual misconduct. And they are certainly not generally aware of what actions to take, what redress is possible, or which persons to contact when they have been harassed or abused, even if the victim has the courage to disclose.

Perhaps most important, in many cases the level of fear that religious leadership has with respect to its own prosecution for similar offenses, is inversely proportional to the speedy provision of effective interventions. In this way, denominational disconnectedness has a tendency to enable the perpetuation of abuse. Or to place it in a more piercing metaphor, at the present time, the river of justice is still full of piranha.

SUMMARY

Victims become involved through one of three mechanisms: they are physically forced or are coerced into compliance through the use of the perpetrator's power of position and then pressed into secrecy; they respond to the lure of transference love, are trapped by their own loyalty, and are taken advantage of by the clergyperson; or they seem to willingly go along with inappropriate advances because of an intuitive fear of saying "no" that is a sequel of early-childhood abuse.

Victims do not disclose their abuse for one or several of four major reasons: loyalty and the fear of the loss of a treasured supportive relationship; felt guilt, often as the result of being scapegoated or abused in their families of origin; an intuition that they will not be believed, with consequent congregational retribution and abandonment; and overwhelming fear and denial, often as a response to consciously suppressed childhood victimization or severe anxiety over job or vocational security.

Persons known to the perpetrator, who have either been witness to the abuse or who have knowledge of it, are especially vulnerable to coercive attacks and terrorism by that individual, in the service of keeping the secret. For these secondary victims, there is currently no legal redress nor compensation safety net, and in most cases no procedural protocol for prosecution within the religious institution.

Seminarians, student clergy, and junior ordained staff are the most vulnerable victims because the completion of their ordination processes and job placement often depend on the favorable evaluation and recommendation of clergy abusers.

False accusation is a rare phenomenon, because of the attendant repercussions of disbelief, disenfranchisement, scapegoating, isolation, and abandonment by the family of faith that are likely to ensue.

Finally, religious institutions, long governed by the "old boy" network rather than ethical codes, have not yet risen adequately to the need for established, published, ethical standards and adequate protocols for the protection of primary and secondary victims, as well as the prosecution of perpetrators. Those institutions that have begun to formulate and publish ethical codes and sexual misconduct protocols most often do not make that material readily available to the ordinary congregant or even to individuals in the ordination process.

Chapter 7

The Scapegoat As the Bearer of Evil

In ancient Hebrew times, on Yom Kippur, the Day of Atonement, once a year the high priest sacrificed a goat as a sin offering for the people. The priest then symbolically laid the sins of the people on the back of a second sacrificial goat and sent it out into the wilderness to die. In this manner, the people were divested of their sins, and the community was considered healed.

> Aaron shall take the two he-goats and let them stand before the Lord at the entrance to the Tent of Meeting; and he shall place lots upon the two goats, one marked for the Lord and the other marked for Azazel. Aaron shall bring forward the goat designated by lot for the Lord, which he is to offer as a sin offering; while the goat designated by lot for Azazel shall be left standing alive before the Lord, to make expiation with it and send it off to the wilderness for Azazel. . . . When he has finished purging the Shrine, the Tent of Meeting, and the altar, the live goat shall be brought forward. Aaron shall lay both his hands upon the head of the live goat and confess over it all the inequities and transgressions of the Israelites, whatever their sins, putting them on the head of the goat; and it shall be sent off to the wilderness through a designated man. Thus the goat shall carry on it all their inequities to an inaccessible region; and the goat shall be set free in the wilderness. (Lev 16:7-22)[1]

It is particularly interesting that according to Jewish legend,[2] Azazel was originally an angel, and once on the Day of Atonement he accused Israel before God, saying, "Why hast thou mercy on them when they provoke thee?" In short, Azazel was of the opinion that God's role was judgment, not mercy. To this God replies, " If thou wouldst be amongst them (men), thou wouldst also sin." That is, *You grandiose being, if you weren't an angel, you would also be tempted, and sin.* According to the legend, Azazel didn't get it, and so he asked to be tested. With God's permission he descended to earth and now with mortal vulnerability promptly lusted after Noah's wife, Na'amah, a very beautiful woman. As a result of his sin and his audacity, God then said, "Since he sinned and cannot return to heaven, he should remain in the desert until the end of time, so that he should close the mouths of accusers; for they will be warned by his fate, and will be silent." Thence forth Azazel was known as the seducer to sensuality. The scapegoat, bearing the sins of the people, is therefore annually sent to the dwelling place of the fallen angel in the desert in order to remind those who believe God should not show mercy to everyone that Azazel's fate, and therefore theirs, is to be forever barred from heaven.

This legend does several things. First, it reiterates that God's mercy is as important as God's judgment.[3] This is very important to keep in mind with respect to the material that we have been discussing. It is very easy to judge the acts of others as bad, but judgment alone does not facilitate the process of healing.

Second, the legend recognizes sexuality and sensuousness as having more power than we usually accord it. With respect to sexual misconduct, we are dealing with more than the drive toward procreation. We are encountering the deepest human need, no matter how twisted the expression—the need for safety, security, and nurturance.

Finally, and of particular interest to this chapter, is that the scapegoat is an individual who, in a true sacrificial manner, is chosen to bear the sins of the people and be driven out of the community for doing so. And, rather than suffer a quick death by having its throat cut by the priest's knife, the scapegoat is doomed to wander in a parched desolation, eventually suffering a lingering death from thirst and starvation. Most paradoxical, the purpose of all this is to remind those who would judge another harshly that they also are not without sin, and mercy is the better way.

Although today's communities of faith no longer practice ritual animal sacrifice for the absolution of sins,[4] we often do it in an unconscious and metaphoric way—a practice that originates in, and has been modeled from, the families of origin of the member con-gregants. This phenomenon, which we now call *scapegoating,* is common in families that have problems with power and direct confrontation.

SCAPEGOATING IN FAMILIES

Scapegoating in families involves a process called triangulation. Often the victim is, oddly enough, willing, and his or her attraction or attention-getting behavior is symbolic of the larger problem in the system. Scapegoats are carefully selected to meet the needs of the system, and the long-term effects for the chosen individual are significant and of long duration.

Triangulation

From the study of family systems, we know that the relationship between dyads, or pairs of persons, such as marital partners, is often strengthened by co-opting in a third member upon whom can be deflected the anger and rage that results from helplessness, fear, intimidation, and angst in general. This is called *triangulation,* and its intuitive purpose is to remove the tension from directly between the marital pair and thereby diminish the risk of the partners quit-ting the relationship. Most often, the object of this triangulation is a child because children, by nature of their necessary dependence, are functionally less powerful and therefore least threatening and less likely to seek retribution.

The Willing Victim

Children sometimes willingly, albeit unconsciously, participate in the triangulation because they intuitively seek to maintain the integrity of the marital pair. That is, most kids would very much like to have both a mommy and a daddy, and preferably their birth mommy and daddy. They do this by acting out in some way that seems to justify drawing the parental rage, or at least attention. Children from a troubled marriage might steal, break store windows, fail in school, get drunk, or do any number of behaviors that might be seen as unacceptable in order to draw the focus of their parents away from the marital tension and dissatisfaction. Interestingly enough, preacher's kids (PKs) are famous for this sort of behavior.

When there is a power imbalance in the relationship, it is a lot easier to talk about Junior's problem than it is for *me to talk to you* about how angry I am at having to beg for money or for being used like a rug and otherwise treated disrespectfully. It is also easier to talk about Junior's problem than it is to acknowledge that I am responsible for the pain of my partner. If triangulated children are successful at their task of being the *identified patient*, they get their parents into therapy, hopefully with a family therapist who understands what is going on. Sometimes, it is only in this way that mercy happens.

Symbolic Behavior

The scapegoat's negative, attention-drawing behavior is not a random choice. There is always a symbolic or parallel relationship to the real source of the tension in the family. For example, the child may be berated for not participating in school activities or doing poorly in sports. The real issue, however, may be the father's fear or lack of desire to participate in any sort of social engagement or his failed athletic career. In another case, the parents may focus on the child's shoplifting, while the real issue is the mother's need to keep up with the Joneses, which is causing financial distress to the family. Or, the child may be berated as being too fat, which is really a projection of the mother's unhappiness with her own body. Of particular note is the parental complaint that a child is a liar, when the real problem is that the family is invested in keeping one or more secrets. We will deal more with the destructive nature of secrets in the next chapter.

Selection and Induction of Scapegoats

Various forces come into play in the selection and induction of an individual into the scapegoat role. In families, birth order is often important. Family expectations often fall heavily on the firstborn child or firstborn, male child, and as such it is easy for these children to fail to live up to their parents' wishful desires, especially if the parent or parents have not felt successful in their own lives. In this situation, the child or young adult can never be good enough. Over-identification of a parent with a same-sex child can have a similar effect, as the parent tries to angrily mold the child into the parent's ideal image. When a marital relationship is unnurturing, parents often "pick" one of their children with whom they are overattentive. Then, reversing the family hierarchy, they use that child both as a source of companionship and emotional support and as a shield against the insults of their adult partner. This is often called *symbolic incest*. Needless to say, the left-out partner feels betrayed by, or at least in competition with, that particular child, who then has a difficult time doing anything right in the outsider parent's eyes. This is a particularly common scenario in blended families, where tight dyads often form between a custodial parent and his or her child prior to remarriage.

Long-Term Effects

Unfortunately, when the scapegoating has been of long duration, the child often feels responsible for the family pain, leading to a poor self-image and significant depression. The child actually wears or accepts the negative projection/picture of the parents as really being the stuff of what he or she is made. She is a slut, selfish, a thief, and he is a liar, lazy, and incompetent. The child also may have difficulty leaving the family and launching his or herself as an adult. This is because of a felt but unconscious loyalty to being the buffer between the marital pair. This loyalty is reinforced by a strong sense of guilt and additional family messages that mark the young adult as "bad" for seeking a life outside the childhood home and abandoning the parents. Should the young adult successfully launch him or herself and leave the nest, it is not uncommon for a second child, and then even a third, to assume the scapegoat role.

Finally, and of particular importance to this discussion, the child may develop the lifelong pattern of unconsciously re-creating the scapegoating pattern in his or her environment. Every time an important relationship is threatened, the individual may seek to draw the negative energy to his or herself, thereby defusing the tension but at a personal cost. The child may actually develop the expectation that his or her lot is to suffer, much like the saints and martyrs. The child may gradually acquire a high degree of tolerance to emotional pain, causing the individual in adult years to minimize the effect of trauma, both to themselves and when and if they report it to others.

SCAPEGOATING IN COMMUNITIES

Scapegoating is always the projection of one's own hostility or the group's hostility on to another. Like the ancient people of Israel who sacrificed animals to appease God for their sins, we also sacrifice, not ourselves but someone else, in order to be rid of the guilt of our misdeeds and the fear and interior hostility that would rend the fabric of our community. We create an enemy by choosing someone who is different or unknown to us, when the enemy is really ourselves. And when we feel fractured, we unite ourselves in opposition to others. It would seem that in our culture we have created a generation of victims as a result of our corporate felt sense of powerlessness.

When Different Is Bad

Communities often scapegoat persons or groups of persons who are unknown or different. We do this because either they make us feel insecure, or because they are an easy target.

As was mentioned earlier, we often replace feelings of insecurity and fear with feelings of anger because being pumped up with aggressive energy has more survival value than being paralyzed with fright. We are often uneasy about strangers when we do not understand them, or their ways, and therefore cannot predict their behavior. Or, we are afraid when in some way the behavior or beliefs of strangers seem to run against our established norms, perhaps bringing them into question. We fear that either they will break our "rules" or that we will break their "rules," and they will seek retribution. Strangers may also seem to have the freedom to do things that we have denied ourselves. This latter may be one reason that divorced people were shunned and shamed for so long in the United States. It certainly is the grounds for what we call homophobia, or the fear and scapegoating of gay persons, particularly by those who are, at some level, in conflict with their own sexual identity.

Second, when persons are essentially unknown to us, they are as a blank screen onto which it is easy for us to project our own anger, hostility, and judgment, which up until that point we had directed at ourselves. When we do this, we are relieved because the problem is now "out there" instead of "in here." Jesus of Nazareth spoke to our tendency to do this when he said:

> Or how can you say to your brother, 'Let me take the speck out of your eye,' when there is the log in your own eye? You hypocrite, first take the log out of your own eye, and then you will see clearly to take the speck out of your brother's eye. (Mat 7:4-5) (RSV)

United (Against a Common Enemy) We Stand

It is not uncommon for communities to define and unite themselves in opposition to others. "We are free people, not like those communists." "We are people of the *true* God, not like those heathens who are going to hell." It is almost as if, in the absence of the "enemy," we have no identity of our own. For North Americans, the Russians served this purpose for years, and when the Cold War ended, it seemed for a time as if we weren't sure what it meant to be American. Were we separate ethnic strains, and should Spanish be accepted as our second language and used as such in our schools, or were we truly combined in the "melting pot?" One might hypothesize that one of the reasons for the popularity of the recent war in the Mideast, Operation Desert Storm, was that once again we had a scapegoat and could rally in opposition. Somehow Saddam Hussein and his warriors were just what we needed in order to proudly parade around with American flags waving from the back of our pickup trucks.

One of the qualities of a community scapegoat is that the person or persons in question become mythologized and perhaps even turned into a "thing." To the Nazis, the Jewish people became conspiring, blood-sucking money-mongers who had bankrupted and threatened the demise of the "Aryan" nation. During World War II, the Japanese soldiers ceased being people and became "gooks." African Americans have been and, by some white Americans, still are called "niggers," characterized as slothful, stupid, thieving, good-for-nothings. Pro-lifers shoot and kill persons who espouse the Pro-choice position because they consider them to be subversive murderers. Not only are negative attributes generalized and placed upon persons as a group, but there is usually little real data to support the accusations. More important, it becomes clear in the group or in the majority mind that we are good and they are bad.

A Generation of Victims

As we have seen, to the extent that communities are engaged in scapegoating, it lets the group members off the hook when it comes to confessing and addressing their own internal problems. The problem is always "over there." Twenty years or so ago in the United States, our legal system exacerbated this problem of finger-pointing. We reinterpreted the tort law such that any injured party was considered eligible for due compensation, regardless of whether or not the person was at fault for not using reasonable precaution. Just a minor example of this is the disappearance of diving boards from the marketplace, because some persons who choose to jump off them have injured themselves and subsequently successfully sued the manufacturers. Many obstetricians have closed their practices because clients and the courts have held them responsible for every possible thing that can go wrong with a newborn, including low birth weight (often the result of smoking), and fetal alcohol syndrome. The list is legion. Prudence and art are no longer positions that can be defended. When we are hurting, it must be someone else's fault. When we are hurting, we make the assumption that we have been victimized instead of entertaining the possibility that we misjudged, were negligent, or even that grace, somehow, was operative.

A victim, by definition, is helpless. When we decide that *we* are the victim, instead of that bad person or group, we see ourselves as being in a powerless position. And, as a result of seeing ourselves as the victim, we are able to divest ourselves of the responsibility for changing ourselves or the system. Then we can say, "African Americans are lazy thieves, therefore I don't have to exert any effort to ameliorate the damage done to their persons and society by myself and my ancestors." Like the angel, Azazel, we judge the other without looking first at ourselves. We find them wanting without taking responsibility for our own predispositions and involvement.

SCAPEGOATING IN CONGREGATIONS

Congregations select scapegoats in much the same way and for the same reasons that families and communities select scapegoats. Congregations that feel insecure or have a sense of disunity, congregations that have an inner tension and poor conflict resolution skills, or congregations that have an unhappy secret such as clergy misconduct, often unconsciously seek out a scapegoat on whom to lay the evil. The scapegoat, in turn, is either sacrificed or chased out into the desert in hopes that the community will be cleansed. The target for this unfortunate phenomenon may be a particular group or member of the congregation or a clergyperson, chosen because his or her behavior or position is symbolically parallel to the problem. It may be the messenger who discloses clergy misconduct, or it may be the primary, or secondary victims of clergy sexual abuse or harassment. "Afterpastors," clergypersons who follow the tenure of an individual who engaged in clergy sexual misconduct, are frequent scapegoats and secondary victims.

The Scapegoat As the Carrier of Symbolic Guilt

Sometimes persons or particular groups within a congregation find themselves scapegoated because they are in the wrong place at the wrong time. There is something about them, or something about what they do that causes a negative association in the minds of the membership of a conflicted congregation. In short order they find that they have become a lightning rod for the tension, and they get burned by the current. An example of this would be the chairperson of the pastoral search committee who is accused of moving too quickly or of facilitating the selection of an improper candidate, when the real issue is the unresolved grief of the congregation for a suddenly departed, beloved spiritual leader. Or, it might be the feminist, gay, or even conservative members of the congregation who receive underground animosity because the family of faith, as a result of its theological diversity and fear of outright anger, is unable to discuss beliefs and values. In this case, these persons may be reduced to impersonal "things" and should the conflict reach the point of crisis, the congregation may seek unification and a sense of identity at the cost of part of its membership.

Again, it is easier to scapegoat than it is to address the real issue. The problem is usually not solely due to a lack of courage on the part of the congregants. Most often there is a real lack of conflict-resolution skills because, as we have seen, they have not been modeled in the families of origin of the membership.

"Afterpastors,"[5] or clergypersons who succeed colleagues who have engaged in financial or sexual pastoral misconduct, often find themselves scapegoated, particularly when the misconduct is a "family" secret. While trying their level best, but unaware of the original betrayal, they discover themselves the target of blame and mistrust. In particularly difficult cases, where the congregation is still trying to preserve their illusion of the perfect family, afterpastors may become the focus of the rage that the members of the congregation are unwilling to admit exists. These clergy successors are unable to do anything wholly acceptable, finding themselves constantly triangulated in disputes and caught in a mill of mixed messages such as, "We want to grow, but we do not want to change," "You are our savior, but you aren't doing anything right," and "You are supposed to lead, but you don't respect our authority." As a result, the tenure of afterpastors is frequently short and the rate of burnout, high.

Killing the Messenger

As has been discussed, congregations frequently tenaciously cling to their image of the happy family. Persons who would shatter this illusion are therefore often seen as the enemy. People and congregations frequently do not want to see their face in the mirror, especially if they are feeling ashamed of something. In this case, not unlike the unhappy stepmother in the fairy tale, *Snow White*, it is more comfortable for the congregation to shatter the mirror. An example of mirror-shattering might be the congregation that felt guilty about its treatment of a terminated leader and instead of confronting the reasons for their conflict with that leader, scapegoated the church historian who recorded the incident.

In the case of clergy misconduct, the person or persons who disclose the matter to the congregation, be they the afterpastor, the lay leadership, or the judicatory, will often find themselves blamed for being unfair or having ulterior motives. In one case, concerned congregational members who finally came forward and disclosed evidence of pastoral misconduct were publicly disclaimed and accused of lying by the lay leadership, even though the leadership was aware of the misbehavior of the clergyperson in question. In another, threats were made against the life of an afterpastor who got too close to the shameful truth regarding the secret but flagrant sexual behavior of a former colleague, who involved himself both with minors and several of the significant lay leaders. Often, fear on the part of fiscally responsible congregational leaders—that such disclosure might mean the loss of a charismatic preacher who has been successful at reaping revenue for the treasury—may also drive a scapegoating movement.

Scapegoating the Victim

In cases of disclosed pastoral sexual misconduct, adult victims are frequently, if not almost always scapegoated by at least a portion, if not the majority of the congregation. Because it is unbearable to believe that the beloved spiritual leader/good object could commit such acts, since that would shatter the fantasy that one had at last found the ultimate caregiver, victims are often unforgivable. This of course is also true in incestuous families, where the victimized child is often attacked by uninvolved siblings, as well as a nonparticipating parent(s) or a parent who does not want to remember his or her own childhood sexual abuse. Frequently this offensive is also fueled, in part, by fear of economic disadvantage should the abuser be jailed or removed by court order from the home, or in the case of congregations, fail to be able to preach on Sunday.

In both congregations and families, double jeopardy and particularly vicious attacks may occur when there has been undisclosed abuse in prior pastorates or generations. This is a result of the entrenched denial that has protected the earlier secret and now fears that all will be unveiled. Similarly, other clergy colleagues may assault, or at least try to undermine the victim in their over-identification with the perpetrator and anxiety that similar incidents in their own past might come to light.

Most often victims are accused of lying; having a grudge against the pastor, or some ulterior motive; being seductive and trapping the pastor, much like Pharaoh's wife; being sick, neurotic, or needy; or simply being evil. Victims are most often seen as one-dimensional and through labeling are frequently turned into impersonal things, making it easier to emotionally abuse and kill them.

Scapegoating Secondary Victims of Sexual Misconduct

There are many secondary victims of clergy misconduct, including the aforementioned afterpastors, the families of victims and of the offending clergyperson, the betrayed congregation, clergy as a disgraced professional group, and besmudged religious institutions at large.[6] All of these groups are vulnerable to scapegoating. However, foremost among these are the spouses of the clergy perpetrators. Very often clergy wives are scapegoated for not "being there" sufficiently for their husbands or not being a good-enough wife. It is easier for the congregation to blame the wife than it is for the membership to let go of their illusion of their perfect caregiver, or even take responsibility for treating the clergyperson poorly themselves. Most often, congregations consider that they hire the clergyperson to take care of them and then leave it up to God to take care of the clergyperson. This is not responsible community and leaves the spiritual leader isolated, lonely, unsupported, and vulnerable to the temptation to look for that support in inappropriate places.

THE PRICE THEY PAY:
THE DESTRUCTIVE EFFECTS OF SCAPEGOATING

Although it might appear obvious, little thought is often given to the painful—even permanently painful—effects of being scapegoated. These individuals may suffer significant physical as well as psychological symptoms of being targeted in this way. Furthermore, psychological insult also has spiritual effects, and scapegoating may lead to a loss of faith. Finally, scapegoated persons may be led into their role as a result of their experience in their families of origin, and the congregational scapegoating then becomes a piggyback insult that has the potential of destroying the individual.

A Thorn in the Flesh

Humans are body, mind, and spirit—one entity undivided—and as such, psychological insult often results in physical manifestations. Scapegoated individuals often suffer symptomatic health problems. Headaches, rashes, chronic fatigue, and high blood pressure have been reported by one researcher.[7] Other symptoms that commonly occur are frequent colds and sinus conditions, due to a stress-induced depression of the immune system; serious gastrointestinal symptoms; and neck, back, and general muscle pain. Significant depression and anxiety along with related insomnia is also common. These conditions may become serious and chronic and significantly affect the individual's general ability to function.

The Parched Desert

Psychological insult also has spiritual effects. When an individual is scapegoated, he or she loses the support of the community of faith and suffers abandonment, loss, loneliness, and isolation. The bond of trust between the individual and the community is ruptured, and the scapegoat is driven out of the garden where God is experienced. The person becomes spiritually homeless and often hopeless, because the body of belief, the values that bound and connected the individual to the community, have been violated. As in the case of Job, life may no longer make sense, and the scapegoated person may lose his or her foundation—the ground upon which meaning is built. This of course can be transformational, but more often scapegoating can be a crisis that kills faith.

Becoming the Image of Evil

Family of origin experiences may predispose individuals to be chosen for the scapegoat role. Children who grow up in the scapegoat triangle often suffer from the whole spectrum of psychological maladies. One of the reasons for this is that they are given continual feedback, both verbally and nonverbally, that they are wrong, bad, guilty, and generally fall short of social standards. They see themselves as negative people, even unpersons with no right to be, unredeemable. In addition, in order to contain their anxiety and retrieve some sense of control in an abusive situation, small children often engage their native creativity in intrapsychic mind-bending. They trick themselves into imagining that they, the children, are the bad persons rather than their giant caretakers, and if only they would change, everything would be all right. This becomes what is called an *early childhood decision,* and once made, slips into unawareness and forever after affects the behavior of the individual. One of the most painful aspects of this process, as is well-documented in child abuse cases, is that mistreated, even physically beaten children will return again and again to the parent in the undying hope of being forgiven by the one person who should love them.

This pattern is often continued into adulthood. Adults who have been scapegoated as children will unconsciously seek out persons, situations, and perhaps congregations in which they will again be scapegoated, in order that they might again, in this strange way, have the opportunity to seek redemption. They will be incredibly loyal to the cause, and in our case to the congregational family, in spite of their abuse. This process is reflected in Charles Dickens, *A Tale of Two Cities,* in which the hero, Sydney Carton, an odd double of an individual despised by the French Revolutionaries, allows himself to be taken and guillotined in the man's stead. As Carton stands on the platform above the murderous crowd, awaiting his death:

> They said of him, about the city that night, that it was the peacefullest man's face ever beheld there. Many added that he looked sublime and prophetic. If he had given an utterance to his (thoughts) they would have been these . . .

> "I see that child who lay upon her bosom (the wife of the man he saved) and who bore my name, a man winning his way up in that path of life which once was mine. I see him winning it so well, that my name is made illustrious there by the light of his. I see the blots I threw upon it, faded away. I see him, foremost of just judges and honored men, bringing a boy of my name, with a forehead that I know and golden hair, to this place—then fair to look upon, with not a trace of this day's disfigurement—and I hear him tell the child my story, with a tender and faltering voice.

It is a far, far better thing that I do, than I have done; it is a far, far better rest that I go to, than I have ever known."[8]

It is an interesting exercise to wonder how many of our martyrs were groomed for the role by being scapegoated by their families.

SUMMARY

The concept *scapegoat* originates in ancient Hebrew times in the cultic ritual of the Day of Atonement. The scapegoat was the second part of a two-part sacrifice that was designed to divest the religious community of its sins and thereby heal it. The Jewish legend, or Midrash, that surrounds the biblical story of the scapegoat reiterates that mercy is as important as judgment, sex has more power than we usually accord it, and that the scapegoat is an individual who in sacrifice points to the accusers and warns them of an impending eternal rupture of their right relationship with God.

Families that have power imbalances, particularly between the marital pair, often seek to diffuse rage and fear and thereby stabilize themselves by engaging in *triangulation*. The triangulated individual, always a less powerful person and usually a child, is then targeted by the family as the cause of the problem and therefore the "bearer of sin" that we call the scapegoat. In this process, children are often willing victims because of their intuitive desire to maintain the integrity of the family unit. The selection and induction of the scapegoat is not random; it usually has significance that is symbolic to the underlying tension in the family and may be facilitated by birth order or physical traits. The long-term effects upon scapegoated children often make it difficult for them to free themselves to live independent adult lives.

Communities also tend to project their own fear and hostility onto others when there is tension, disunity, and a lack of conflict-resolution skills within the group. Communities frequently choose as their scapegoats persons or groups who are unknown or different because difference parallels their own disunity, and the unknown provides a convenient blank screen upon which to project hostility, turning it into the problem "out there" instead of "in here." In this way, it is not unusual for communities to unite themselves against a perceived common enemy. In North America, partially because of the current functioning of our legal system, we have become a generation of finger-pointers and professional victims, who out of our felt helplessness, divest ourselves of the responsibility for changing destructive social systems.

Congregations select scapegoats the same way families and communities do. Congregations that feel insecure or have a sense of disunity, congregations that have an inner tension and poor conflict-resolution skills, or congregations that have an unhappy secret, such as clergy sexual misconduct, often unconsciously seek out a scapegoat upon which to lay the evil. Families of faith also select scapegoats because they symbolically, by their behavior or position, represent the unresolved issue that the membership is struggling with. Afterpastors figure prominently in this group. Because congregations frequently tenaciously cling to their image of the happy family, they may also scapegoat persons who disclose the family secret or the reason for the congregational conflict. Finally, primary and secondary victims of clergy sexual misconduct are frequently scapegoated by at least a portion, if not the majority of the congregation because, for many, it is unbearable to believe that the beloved spiritual leader/ good object could commit such acts.

Scapegoats suffer physically and mentally as a result of this sort of abuse. Because a scapegoated individual(s) loses the support of the community of faith and suffers abandonment, loneliness, isolation, and often a questioning if not shattering of values, scapegoating can be a crisis that kills faith. A person who has been scapegoated in his or her family of origin receives piggyback pain because of the tendency of these individuals to grow up with the sense that they are wrong, bad, guilty, and generally fall short of social standards. These persons, in their attempt to contain anxiety, often have made the early-childhood decision that they are the problem, even that they themselves are evil. In their unconscious attempt to seek redemption, they are fiercely loyal not only to the their family of origin but also to the congregation and community, returning again and again to be martyred for the cause.

Chapter 8

Untold Tales
and Skeletons in the Closet

Hurtful behaviors are often perpetuated in religious systems through the keeping of family secrets. When abuse or other inappropriate behavior is covered up, or the congregation is unwilling to recognize its presence, the causes cannot be addressed. As we have discussed, congregations may choose secrecy when the reputation or removal of a beloved or a crowd-drawing pastor is at stake, or when something has happened that could shatter the illusion of the perfect family, and/or cause open conflict. In these instances, confidentiality is often confused with secrecy.

Confidentiality comes from a Latin root that means to "place trust in," while secrecy comes from a Latin root that means "hidden." Confidentiality in these contexts is an ethical obligation on the part of a professional, be it clergyperson, counselor, physician, or lawyer, to not reveal the contents of privileged communication except upon the permission of the client or the order of a court, where binding. Privileged communication is information that passes between a client, or a parishioner, and one of the above sorts of professionals *in the context of the ordinary duties of a defined professional relationship.* Furthermore, *the client is not bound by the rules of confidentiality, as they apply only to the professional*, the person in whom the client put his or her trust.

The rule of secrecy, on the other hand, is not binding upon the perpetrator, the person of power and often a professional, but upon the victim or victims. Secrecy is a hidden truth about ruptured trust.

PANDORA'S BOX

The keeping of secrets in a family or a congregation is similar to the story of Pandora and her box. However, in this case, the process of keeping the lid on the box is actually more injurious than its contents.

The Gifts of the Gods

The Greek myth of Pandora's box, although rather unkind to women,[1] is an apt metaphor for the congregation that contains an ugly secret. According to this myth, the God Zeus, who is the head of the Greek pantheon, is displeased because of the actions of Prometheus, one of the gigantic race of Titans who inhabited the earth before the creation of humankind. Prometheus and his brother Epimetheus had been charged with the creation of man, who was to be a nobler being than the animals. In order to fulfill his task, Prometheus took some of the newly created earth, which still contained some divine seeds, and kneading it with water made man in the image of the gods. But then he was sorry for man because all the good gifts—swiftness, and the ability to soar in the sky, sharp smell and acute hearing, endurance and warm, furry coverings—had been given to the animals. So Prometheus took it upon himself to steal the sacred fire from heaven and bring it to man. No longer would man have to shiver, for he could use the fire to warm his dwellings and cook his food, as well as fashion tools and weapons to protect himself.

But even beyond this, Prometheus felt that men toiled too hard to provide for themselves, so he tricked Zeus and taught men how to steal the best part of the sacrificial offerings for themselves and leave only the fat and bone for the gods. Zeus was not happy. He dealt harshly with Prometheus, but that is another story.

Not only was Zeus angry at Prometheus, but he was also jealous of the fortune of man, so he decided to punish them for accepting the gift of fire and for cheating the gods. He created a beautiful woman, the first woman, also out of clay and water, and the gods followed suit by imbuing her with every grace. Aphrodite, the goddess of love, gave her beauty. Hermes, the god of trade, gave her skill in speech and reasoning. Apollo, the god of the arts, gave her a love of music. The Three Graces gave her charm and spirit. Zeus called her "Pandora," which means "every gift." Then he gave her one more favor, the gift of curiosity. He sent her to earth to find a husband, and with her he sent a golden box, which he instructed her never to open.

Hermes brought Pandora down to earth and offered her to Epimetheus, who could not resist the beautiful woman and took her as his wife. Pandora began her life happily but eventually became bored and restless. One day when her husband was away, her curiosity got the best of her. Taking out the box, she cracked open the lid. The top flew up and out swirled a multitude of plagues for hapless man—gout, rheumatism, disease, envy, spite, revenge, and fear. Pandora tried to slam the cover closed, but alas, only one thing was left in the box, something silvery on the bottom. When her husband returned home, it was quite clear from the odd, suddenly destructive behavior of his neighbors that something awful had happened. Pandora showed him the box and tearfully told him what she had done. Then she remembered there was still something else in the box. Again she opened the lid, and this time, there, lying on the bottom, her curiosity discovered silvery Hope.

Human beings can consider a great variety of things to be bad or shameful, with the resultant wish to hide them. Dr. Kate Wachs, a family therapist in Chicago says of secrets, "When things are hidden, they become so much more powerful. Each time you lie about it, you are telling yourself that it is a terrible thing. And then when you look at it, it usually turns out that it is not so bad."[2] On the downside, as one victim of a family secret said, "Secrets don't work. Eventually the truth comes out, and all there is left is the pain."[3]

Like Pandora's box, congregations are often containers of all sorts of secrets. In the case of clergy misconduct, they will also be containers of not only abuse, but distrust, anger, fear, betrayal, paralysis, and a legion of other diseases. Unlike Pandora, however, congregants are for the most part not curious about the contents and wish the lid to remain tightly closed. In fact, they punish anyone who would reveal the contents for fear that the family of faith will be harmed. They enforce a "zone of silence" around undiscussable matters, creating odd gaps in communication and record keeping. One congregation became so entrenched in this process that it stopped keeping records of baptisms, confirmations, marriages, and deaths of its members! As family therapist Evan Imber-Black of the Albert Einstein College of Medicine in New York says, "Sometimes everyone knows the secret, but the unspoken rule is we're not allowed to know we know."[4] What the family of faith doesn't understand is that the evils work their misery even while still contained in the box. But Hope, unless freed, cannot do its healing work.

Keeping the Lid On

Returning to a bit of English etymology, the words "secret" and "security" come from the same root. In Chapter 2 we talked about *highly defended religious systems,* congregations that maintain a protective wall about themselves to ward off societal judgment and an inner wall of denial, rationalization, and repression that protects the members from realities that are too harsh to bear. These defenses might be seen as secrets from the world and secrets from the self— ways to maintain a sense of outer and inner security and "keep the lid on." These congregations are afraid that if the secret gets loose, the congregation or its individual membership will be destroyed.

The keeping of a secret produces more pain to more people than the original insult itself. This is because while the original wounding may have been a single incident or have involved a single victim, the keeping of the secret inevitably, over time, involves many people and repeated incidents of the above secret-keeping behaviors. One wound can become the affliction of many.

It has been said that a secret is something that you tell one person at a time. Secrets leak. They leak from the mouths of the consorts of celebrities; they leak from legal proceedings into the press; they leak from insiders in the FBI; they leak from "confidential" insurance company health records; and they leak from one parishioner to the next. Secrets shared in this way develop a life of their own. Much of their substance is *hearsay,* or material that someone heard from somewhere and repeated to someone else. Like the game "Pass It On," where a group of players sit in a circle and one whispers a sentence to his or her neighbor, who in turn whispers it to his or her neighbor, the end result often has little similarity to the original thought or action. Yet, because the matter is a "secret" the validity of the content cannot be "checked" or verified.

Over time, as the contents of the secret continue to mutate, victims as well as perpetrators may be ascribed inaccurate histories and imbued with characteristics that either vilify or overidolize them. When one is vilified and the other overidolized, a scapegoat is created. In addition, persons who for any reason are uncomfortable with the secret have to be kept in line, which most often occurs through various acts of coercion, isolation, or even terrorism, the mode and effect of which will be discussed in the next section.

A frequently observed pattern, usually resulting from clergy misconduct, is the *clergy killer congregation.* These congregations express the pain of their organizational distress through a history of short-term pastorates and an air of anticlericalism. When the family secret involves sexual misconduct, it is particularly toxic. Perhaps this is because sex, in our society, has greater taboos surrounding it than money. Certainly, in ancient Israel, adultery was punishable by death—albeit mostly for women—and incest was punishable either by death or by complete and permanent separation from the community. Theft, however, was a lighter crime and was punishable by the payment of double or severalfold damages, depending upon the nature of the misappropriation.

Family and congregational secrets are kept in many ways. For purposes of this discussion, the mechanics of secret keeping will be divided into two parts: institutional patterns and psychological dynamics. Institutional patterns are observable group behaviors that repeat themselves. They originate as an unaware or intuitive response to an event or events, and even though they may be destructive or counterproductive, they are the community's traditional choice for dealing with certain situations. On the other hand, psychological dynamics might be seen as the intrapsychic and interpsychic processes that occur in the minds of individuals, causing them to act in certain ways toward themselves and toward others. Institutional patterns are the "how" of congregational behavior, and psychological dynamics are the "why." We will deal with the "how" first.

INSTITUTIONAL PATTERNS
AND THE PAINFUL FOOTPRINTS OF A SECRET

A family secret is something that is not openly talked about, and it should be said here that while most family secrets tend to be shameful, unresolved grief is a major exception. Secrets such as grief become secrets simply because talking about them causes family or community members to revisit the pain in ways that they cannot tolerate. As a result, the pain goes underground and is then expressed in a number of usually counterproductive ways. These can include "clergy killing," in this case a pattern that develops as the congregation continually, but unsuccessfully, attempts to replace what it has lost. Since no two persons are the same in every way, replacement, whether it be a spouse, a child, or a clergyperson, is always doomed to dissatisfaction and failure.

However, when sexual misconduct of any type is the skeleton in the family closet, whether it be of short or long duration and whether or not the offending clergyperson left inexplicably or remained for a number of years after the incident, these congregations, not unlike incestuous families, present with a number of predictable patterns of distress. The secret may be closely held by a few main players; the secret may be vaporous and no one may know anything for sure, save for a heavy intuition; or the secret may be a subject of whispered speculation in circles of gossip. Nonetheless, a great deal of energy is used in keeping the lid on Pandora's box, which includes not only the secret but the resultant rage, anger, loss, fear, and shame.

The Reverend Chilton Knudson has written an impeccable and comprehensive article on this subject, titled "Understanding Congregational Dynamics," in the 1995 Alban Institute publication, *Restoring the Soul of a Church.* First we will look at the general course and influence of these congregational protective behaviors, and then we will look at the particular psychological dynamics involved. Then, in the next chapter, we will examine all of this in the light of a case history.

Knudson has characterized the recognizable and repeating behavior patterns of congregations suffering from a history of clergy misconduct as serving one or more of five purposes: to provide a distraction or smoke-screen; to protect the secret; to provide avenues of discharge for underlying rage and anger; to symbolically express, often in distorted ways, the nature of the secret; and to serve as compensation for a diffuse sense of violation and shame.

To Provide a Distraction or Smoke Screen

Distraction and smoke-screen patterns create confusion and uncertainty and delay or evade any processes that would seek to uncover the real problem. They may include persistent confusion about roles, responsibility, and lines of authority, such as the lack of written job descriptions, administrative procedures, or an organizational constitution or flow chart. Weak or absent personnel policies and processes for evaluation, especially of clergy, staff members, or other parish leadership add to the fuzziness, as do rump meetings that seek to sidestep established protocol. Inadequate, edited, or otherwise biased systems of communication, such as a lack of staff or congregational meetings, along with focusing on the trivial and routine, such as plant maintenance and benevolences, also provide an effective screen and diversion. Finally, an absence of public, published, or generally agreed-upon policies with regard to money and mission, along with the display of initial enthusiasm followed by an inability to organize and follow-through with program, complete the characteristic inertia.

To Protect the Secret

These patterns directly shield the secret from discovery, so that it is there, but not there. Defensiveness about a portion of the institution's history, selective amnesia or forgetting of certain events, and the mysterious absence of records or meeting minutes provide an effective veil, as do rules or taboos about discussing certain topics, particularly having to with sex, gender, or relationships. Overidealization of a previous pastor (the person who can do no wrong) and subtle or overt discrediting of persons who have left the religious community (usually the victim or one or more scapegoats), as well as resistance to reaching out to lapsed members, keep the real nature of the secret from coming to light. Fear and avoidance of "story-sharing" programs, where taboo information might be communicated also deters the telling of the truth, as does the unexplained disappearance of a formerly vital program, such as a children's choir or the Women's Fellowship. Such a program may have collapsed because of inner conflict about the event or because the leadership was involved in the secret and either left or was removed.

To Provide Avenues of Discharge for Underlying Rage and Anger

The footprints of anger and rage include scapegoating and blaming the victim; coercive terrorism and verbal abuse by persons who do not want their illusions shattered; withholding of contributions; and stoning the messenger or punishing persons who try to point out destructive behaviors or bring the secret to light. Congregational helplessness and depression, expressed as a lack of energy, difficulty getting going, pervasive sadness, or nostalgia about "the good old days," is indicative of anger turned inward. Outright anger at denominational structures for not doing anything, manipulation, power struggles, and competition amongst leadership are all expressions of helplessness and the rage born of fear. Perhaps the most painful behavior of all is "murder" in the name of caring, or seductive sweetness coupled with intrusive concern and subsequent betrayal of the victim or scapegoat.

To Symbolically Express, Often in Distorted Ways, the Nature of the Secret

Symbolic expression is a common type of behavior in all dysfunctional families and as we have discussed, mirrors the problem in creative ways. These behaviors, similar to bad dreams, intuitively and symbolically point the congregants to the very thing they are trying to put out of mind. Such expressions often come in the form of a sudden obsession with the outside appearance of the worship structure, that is tidying up the outside "walls" or fixing the edifice instead of the congregation. A preoccupation with and/or scapegoating of persons with regard to sexual matters such as the marital status of a clergyperson, inclusive language, and the participation and status of gay and lesbian persons is frequently symbolic of sexual misconduct, as is reenactment of the original insult by the calling of a clergyperson who also offends sexually or violates other ethical norms. Discrimination against divorced people, gender-role rigidity, particularly with regard to the ordination or participation of women in leadership, also points to power problems based in distrust. Likewise, unusually persistent sexual humor or flirtation and naiveté and denial with regard to the possibility of inappropriate sexual activity within the congregational context are representative of the keeping of sexual secrets.

To Serve As Compensation for a Diffuse Sense of Violation or Shame

Shame-based congregations are families of faith with a "shadow" created by acts of violation. Because we are often brought up to believe that we are responsible for the actions of others, and therefore all wrong-doing is our personal fault, and because congregants see themselves as members of one body, corporate violation may bring about corporate shame. This shame may be expressed as distrust, suspicion, and hypervigilance, such as excessive concern as to who serves on what committees and excessive concern about the image of the congregation as presented to the outside world. A preoccupation with boundary concerns, what is "ours and theirs" and who gets the keys, along with a usually unconscious discouragement of newcomers, such as a failure to provide adequate parking, help maintain the barriers that protect the family of faith from judging eyes. A preoccupation with doctrinal purity may be symbolic of a felt sense of being dirty. Use of the tactics of guilt to pressure members into making commitments of time or money can be seen as a projection or sharing of shame. And grasping for quick-fix rather than investing in in-depth programs of spiritual or organizational renewal is indicative of a body that does not like what it sees in the mirror. Finally, a tendency to judgmentalism or its polar opposite, laissez-faire irresponsibility, with respect to the evaluation of members and congregational life, is also representative of a body that has judged itself harshly but witholds from itself self-forgiveness.

Congregational Dynamics As Old Bad Habits

Not all of these types of patterns will be demonstrated all the time, but they may occur in any sequence in the ongoing institutional history. Some will be chronic, and some will occur with more severity in times of stress. As in all families, these patterns slip out of consciousness and become "old bad habits" that continue to be repeated and passed down from generation to generation in the congregation, even when the original insult is long past. And, as we have discussed, since families of faith most often do not like seeing their faces in the mirror, particularly when they are secretly certain that they will not enjoy the reflection, they are usually quite defensive about having these problem dynamics pointed out.

The Psychological Dynamics of Secret-Keeping

There are certain psychological dynamics that are worthy of note with respect to the protection of painful or shameful congregational secrets. Coercion, isolation, minimization, repression and denial, deflection and distraction, the distortion of reality, and the invocation of loyalty are the primary drivers of the broader patterns listed in the previous section. "Murder" in the guise of caring is a particularly destructive behavior and also worth examining.

Coercion

Families, since time began, have used emotional abandonment to coerce family members into obeying family rules. By emotionally withdrawing, shutting off conversation, ignoring, or turning a cold, unfeeling side to a recalcitrant or offending member, families and congregations effectively shun or cause these persons "not to be" in a community sense. Offenders, or persons who have broken or would break the secrecy rule thus become disunited from the community, losing their foundation for emotional support. As was discussed earlier, emotional abandonment triggers in most of us instinctive fears that are hard-wired to our struggle for survival. As human infants our incredible vulnerability, as contrasted with the rest of the animal world, makes us extremely dependent upon adult caregivers. In the mind of the infant, withdrawal of support by those caregivers is the first signal of impending physical withdrawal, followed by real and imminent death. We carry this instinct into our adult lives, reinforced, in some cases, by emotional and perhaps even physical abandonment trauma from our childhoods.

Beyond the instinct to survive physically is the instinct to survive spiritually. One might even say that Descartes was somewhat off the mark when he said, "I think therefore I am." Instead, functionally and experientially, perhaps it is more accurate to say *to be is to mean something to someone else*. When meaning born of community and relationship is ruptured, personal meaning and the sense of being alive ceases to exist. This is spiritual death.

Coercion, of course, can be more than the threat of emotional abandonment. It can be the threat of the loss of economic security, a job or position, or even the opportunity to express one's vocation. It can be the threat of public shame and disbelief, the threat of divorce, the threat of public humiliation and/or anger of the members of one's family, or even the threat of physical harm, injury, or death. Coercion can only be practiced by groups or persons that are more powerful, or are perceived of as more powerful, than the target individual. Coercion can take the form of terrorism—individual or group bullying—or it can be a sort of emotional blackmail that takes on evil dimensions. Coercion is most used in shielding the secret and as a way to unload the rage and anger born of fear and shame.

Isolation

Isolation is the natural sequel to emotional abandonment. When one is set apart from the group, pushed out the door so to speak, one is alone. Pressure on the membership by the group or the congregation not to make further contact with the shunned individual results in isolation. Isolation is enforced aloneness. The threat of isolation, or the desire to have the isolation end, brings the individual back into line and enforces the keeping of the secret. When a group acts as a whole, a decision to isolate one or more members on the part of the leadership prevents other group members from making contact and providing the support that might enable the targeted individual to divulge the secret. The same sort of verbal and nonverbal coercion used on these singled-out persons is used on the rest of the group membership to ensure that the leadership directive is obeyed.

Groups or congregations may also isolate targeted members within the walls of the community, much as a solitary cell within a prison. We know from the study of abusive families that the more powerful member or members of such families may seek to isolate one or more of the most vulnerable members, usually the wife or a child. In the case of battering couples, the husband may attempt to isolate the wife from outside support by preventing her from having transportation, a job, or friends. She must then rely solely on the husband for support, giving him ultimate power to abuse her since only by doing his will can she survive. Should she resist, physical death is often the consequence. In the case of incestuous families, children are the members usually isolated. The child, who by reason of his or her physical immaturity cannot drive or transport itself out of the family environment, nor provide for itself in a material way, is also prevented from having outside friends. When older, this child may also be prevented from having a job or having access to transportation or community or after-school activities. This conserves the attention of the child for the abuser, much like confining a woman to a guarded harem. It also prevents the child from gaining the emotional support needed to divulge the secret.

In the case of congregations, targeted individuals may be prevented from making connections with and therefore gaining support from other members within the community. Community members may be told in subtle ways that such and such a person is "untouchable," and interaction with that person will be frowned upon by persons who are important (such as the spiritual leader). The targeted individual may be labeled a troublemaker, or controversial, a poisonous label when placed on a congregational member in the context of a family of faith that is afraid of conflict. Or rumors may be spread about that individual's undesirable behavior, such that anyone coming in contact with him or her is considered likewise tainted. Isolation can only happen when the power of authority, be it the power of individual or of corporate leadership, is greater than the power, or self-perceived power of the targeted member. Isolation is an interruption of communication in the service of protecting or screening the secret.

Minimization, or the Elephant in the Living Room

Minimization is a diminishing of the importance of a reality. As was mentioned previously, persons have been abused or scapegoated in their families of origin either have such a high tolerance for pain, have such a need to repress thoughts of their painful experiences, or feel guilty and at fault themselves that they often minimize the impact of abusive encounters. A sexually molested adult child might say her father was "overly affectionate," or "He didn't really hurt me [because we never had vaginal intercourse]."

Dysfunctional families also diminish the consequence of reality. Partially this is because abusive behavior has become acceptable or unavoidable in the system. However, this is also a way of acknowledging the behavior without telling the secret. A family might say humorously of a pedophilic uncle, "He just likes young flesh."

In similar manner, congregations and victims of clergy sexual misconduct minimize the importance of inappropriate behavior. The victim might say, "He seems to have a crush on me." The congregants might say, "She [the spiritual leader] is unusually friendly," or "He's very charming and seems to be a bit of a ladies' man." Again, this is a way of protecting the perpetrator by acknowledging the behavior but turning it into something not worthy of notice so that the secret is maintained. Minimization is both a screening tactic and a way of coping with shame and guilt.

Repression and Denial

Repression, as has been mentioned before, is the forceful disremembering of traumatic experience. When a vulnerable individual, particularly a child, is caught in an untenable and inescapable situation that causes him or her to engage in an activity that is taboo or otherwise abusive, the individual will often disremember the experience or shove it into a dark, unconscious corner of the mind in order to stave off guilt and anxiety. Sometimes these memories spontaneously return when the individual is sufficiently independent and/or has reached a stage of intrapsychic growth and development that can withstand and process the memory without damage to the self. While repressed, however, the secret is effectively kept, since it has ceased to exist, at least in the mind of the victim.

Members of a congregation can also repress memories of an anxiety-producing incident, such as clergy misconduct. The matter literally passes out of memory in the service of protecting the valued illusion of the happy family, and the secret is effectively kept.

Denial, as we have seen, is a form of personal and corporate dishonesty, a pretending to ourselves that a certain reality does not exist. Denial is the desperate attempt to conceal an awareness, whereas repression is the diminishing of that awareness into unconsciousness. Denial puts the lid on Pandora's box. Repression knows that there is nothing in it. Repression and denial are used directly in the service of keeping the secret, both from oneself and from others.

Deflection and Distraction

Deflection is the redirecting of angry energy from the source of irritation to a safer object, person, cause, or activity. Scapegoating is a form of deflection, as is yelling at our kids after we have had a hard day at work or slamming the door when we are angry at our partner. Deflection can have a domino effect. Dad yells at Mom, Mom picks on the kids, and junior smashes his airplane or kicks the dog. Congregations use deflection when they dump anger on persons of other faiths and beliefs, on afterpastors, on church secretaries, and on victims by finding something "wrong" or "bad" about them.

Distraction is the diversion of blocked or anxious energy into other tasks. As spiritual directors, we commonly see persons who have begun to discern the difficult will of God, get so very busy with myriad worldly tasks that they do not have time to pray. Or as therapists, we often see partners become overinvolved in child-activities or social engagements (or in the case of clergy, parish business), so that they do not have time to think about their marital problems. Distraction is a resource commonly used by families of faith that are trying hard not to look at a problem. Congregations often build buildings, develop mission statements, and revamp programming instead of addressing issues of unresolved grief over the loss of a pastor or unresolved anger at clergy misconduct.

Magic Tricks or the Distortion of Reality

A simple example of the distortion or denial of reality, that as parents we have all probably participated in, is to tell our child, who just scraped his knee in the driveway, that it doesn't really hurt that much. We do this because we are perhaps in a hurry or busy and don't want to take the time to attend fully to the child's needs. Instead we employ the technique of magic healing by getting the child to accept or buy into a reality that works better for us. That is, we try to persuade the child that the injury is minor, or not at all, and nothing to get upset about.

A commonly used way of keeping family secrets is to distort, twist, or deny the reality of the victim so that the victim begins to believe that what he or she experienced, really didn't happen at all. This is done in one of two ways. A person who holds greater power, by reason of status, position, or relationship, suggests to the victim that he or she only imagined the experience, thereby forcing the victim to question his or her reality and perhaps accept the perception of authority.

The second method is even more destructive. More than "brainwashing," one might think of it as "mind rape," the forceful attribution or even insertion of the thoughts and assumptions of a more powerful group or individual into the mind of another. The term denotes a particular kind of violence, as this action entails the violation of the psychic boundaries and personal integrity of a more vulnerable individual by a person or group to whom the individual is in some way subordinate. Mind rape is actually an informal trance phenomenon during which events and agendas are twisted around and the aggressor(s) vigorously insists that either the details of the incident were different or, as a result of the victim's behaviors, he or she was at fault and really the cause of the problem. If the victim was raised in an authoritarian system, where the rule was "theirs not to reply, theirs not to reason why, theirs but to do or die" when under fire in this way, the victim may easily regress to a childlike emotional state. Since obeying authority had survival value as a child, the anxious victim may again do likewise, accepting, or *introjecting* this new version of reality, wholly and uncritically, without the use of appropriate, rational discrimination. This is similar to the way in which one accepts a hypnotic suggestion. Under pressure, the new, distorted reality is substituted for the original experience in the mind of the individual. In this way, the secret is maintained because the incident no longer happened.

This is not uncommon behavior in hierarchical social situations, and because gurus and preachers are usually artful persuaders, they are frequently particularly good at this sort of psychic gymnastic. Needless to say, persons who are subject to this sort of brain-washing begin to feel rather crazy. Of course, this is yet another instance where the imbalance of power enables abuse. And if there is evil, this is certainly high on the list of destructive or dis*graceful* behaviors.

The Invocation of Loyalty

As we discussed in Chapter 1, loyalty is the elevation of group needs above those of the individual member. Loyalty often puts the final lock on the secret. In a world where people grow up in less-than-good-enough holding environments, where employees are turned into objects by product-oriented industry in a market economy, and persons are turned into numbers, we are hungry to be cared for. When nurturing is offered to us, even in the form of a well-done funeral, we are easily and eternally thankful. When we perceive that a family of faith provides us with support that we get nowhere else, we are careful to conserve that community. This is the stuff of which loyalty is made. We are loyal, not only because we are thankful for the sustenance given, but because we hope there will be more. To cut ourselves off from this staff of life, either by breaking the rules or by betraying a secret, becomes unthinkable. As a result, the loyalty to a congregation or to a spiritual leader becomes a substantial obstacle to the disclosure of difficult realities, even if we are not wedded to the illusion of the perfect family. The invocation of loyalty and its protective barriers is the primary way that communities of faith compensate for feelings of violation and shame.

"Murder" in the Guise of Caring

This is probably the most destructive dynamic of all because it comes like a wolf in sheep's—or nurturing parent's—clothing and so represents the ultimate betrayal. The phrase "take care of somebody" should mean something close to "love your neighbor as yourself." However, as attributed to organized crime by the movie media, this same phrase in popular usage means "terminate a life." Frequently found in religious systems because they see themselves as places committed to caring, this activity usually takes the form of pseudosympathetically eliciting details of pain from individuals, and then turning the problem around to make it their fault, or even worse, using the fact of the individual's abuse to implicate and condemn the person. This is the vestry or governing board that listens to a victim's disclosure sympathetically, and then after gleaning many details regarding the individual's past, recommends that he or she should seek counseling because obviously the individual's dysfunctional personal history has impacted significantly on the victim's perception of the present. Or, this is the layleader who in the guise of being emotionally supportive, listens to an abused person's story and then tells the individual and others that the problem is that the victim is angry and therefore is incriminating the perpetrator. This sort of betrayal is the offer of nurturance with the intent to poison, likened to that in the biblical challenge of Luke 11:11-12: "What father among you, if his son asks for a fish, will instead of a fish give him a serpent; or if he asks for an egg, will give him a scorpion?" Here, the author cannot even imagine that a person could be so cruel or uncaring. If there is evil, "murder in the guise of caring" tops the list.

Helplessness and Hopelessness

Congregational depression, often reflected as apathy, results from a condition of helplessness and hopelessness. When too many of the above dynamics are present, people begin to feel crazy, confused, cynical, forsaken, frightened, and powerless. They give up. Hope flies out of the box and is lost. Projects are begun in an effort to rally spirits or create a welcome distraction, but when small obstacles occur, they are abandoned because history has indicated that all efforts are in vain. At this stage, the majority of the congregation has really become the victim, and like the inner-city poor, no longer has the energy to use even those resources that might be available. This stage may mean the end of the community.

INCESTUOUS SYSTEMS AND COLLEGIAL COLLABORATION IN THE SERVICE OF THE SECRET

Finally, it is noteworthy that there are similarities between certain sorts of abusive, dysfunctional congregations and incestuous family systems.[5] This is because these congregations have a parent-child relationship between leadership and membership, and they are closed, or highly defended communities. In many, if not most congregations, there is an intrinsic trust of the clergyperson and his or her intentions, much in the way a child trusts his or her parent. However, in the incestuous system, the community is rigidly authoritarian. There is intrinsic and unequal power between the clergyperson and the congregants as a result of congregational expectation, born of tradition and hierarchical position. This power is amplified by intellectual and educational differences. There is a natural tendency (as a result of God/father transference) for the congregants to obey and please the clergyperson, and there is a psychological vulnerability on the part of individual congregants, particularly when they are in crisis. Ultimately, in these cases, the clergyperson, as with the abusive parent, is wounded and needy, perhaps as a result of early-childhood trauma, and this situation is exacerbated by stress. Added together, these situations are a setup for secrecy, the abuse of power, and clergy sexual misconduct.

Unfortunately, the incestuous system does not stop with the individual congregation but extends to other fearful compatriot clergy outside the parish system but within the clerical "brotherhood," and to the hierarchy of the larger religious institution. Clergypersons often look at the mistakes of their colleagues and think, "There but for the grace of God go I." We can all err, and we can all be sinners. Unfortunately, when clergy *overidentify* with their colleagues, that is, when they regard their peers as being the same as themselves, they often act to protect these persons out of their own need for self-protection. This is the "old boy network," which has now, to some degree, become heterosexual. Furthermore, since clergy tend to be particularly concerned with status and rank, as monetary compensation is not one of the great rewards of ministry, they tend to be very protective of their position and ability to move up in the hierarchy. As in any enterprise (and religion is certainly a business) maintaining the goodwill of profitable connections becomes important. When this reality is coupled with the current general job insecurity of most clerical positions outside of the Roman Catholic Church, it becomes obvious that it is decidedly disadvantageous to undermine one's support system and rat on one's superiors, or even one's peers. It is truly a lonely and prophetic moment when a clergyperson, particularly one of low estate, comes to the conclusion that such an action must be taken.

Ultimately, the weight of the institutional hierarchy has a considerable effect on the disclosure of secrets. Highly placed perpetrators are difficult to confront and dislodge, witness the lengthy histories of misconduct of several North American Roman Catholic and Episcopal bishops of the recent past. Furthermore, the success of disclosing a secret involving clergy misconduct is inversely proportional to the number of persons in the institution who have been involved in the concealment of that, or similar, misconduct. Bluntly, the bigger the coverup and the higher placed the players, the less likely misconduct will be disclosed. This is simply a matter of power in the service of security and the protection of the institution's public image. Victims have had no other recourse but to involve the courts. Although substantial progress has been made in institutional awareness, the realities remain the same.

SUMMARY

The root meaning of confidentiality is "to place trust in," while the root meaning of secrecy is "hidden." Confidentiality is binding upon the professional in the ordinary context of his or her duties, where it provides safety and enables openness within a defined relationship. Secrecy has diffuse boundaries, and it is usually invoked to shield a system or person from guilt, shame, anger, or retribution. It enables abuse and closedness and is binding upon the victim.

The keeping of a secret, over time, causes more pain than does the original insult. This is because the behaviors and energy required to keep a secret in community have significant consequences that create more victims, scapegoats, general confusion, depression, helplessness, and eventual paralysis. In the case of a calamity, such as clergy misconduct, the keeping of the secret becomes a way of life for the congregation. The community begins to develop a whole set of new rules and behavior patterns designed to keep, and cope, with this furtive truth and the patterns that it develops for the most part. These behaviors are intuitive and unconscious designs that may be broken down in five categories: to provide a distraction or smoke screen; to directly protect the secret; to provide avenues of discharge for underlying rage and anger; to symbolically express, often in distorted ways, the nature of the secret; and to serve as a compensation for a diffuse sense of violation and shame.

Secret-keeping patterns involve the use of coercion, isolation, minimization, repression and denial, deflection and distraction, the distortion of reality, the invocation of loyalty, and emotional destruction and betrayal, or "murder" in the guise of caring. Secret-keeping patterns and their underlying psychological dynamics seriously get in the way of the growth and development of religious communities and may even lead to paralysis and dissolution.

Finally, families of faith that have experienced clergy sexual misconduct often share similar dynamics with incestuous family systems. This frequently includes not only the individual congregation but spreads beyond into the greater hierarchy of a denomination through the mechanism of clergy collegial collaboration in the service of the secret. The penchant of religious institutions for a teleological ethical system, which holds the goal as a justification for the means, allows these systems to cover up abuse in order to preserve not only their public image but too often the positions and status of members of the clergy fellowship.

Chapter 9

The Case of Hope Church

Hope Church is a real place, but the names of persons and institutions and some of the details of the incidents have been altered to protect anonymity. This particular case was chosen because, over its long history, this community has manifested most of the patterns of behavior that were discussed in Chapter 8. It is important to remember, however, as we look at this case history that all persons and all institutions make the best possible choices, at the time, with the resources that they have available. Unfortunately, during the period of their development, individuals, families, and institutions frequently come up short in the department of intrapsychic resources and interpersonal skills, particularly those having to do with self-esteem and conflict resolution. As a result, in the struggle to preserve their integrity they do the best they can, which oftentimes is destructive to particular parties, and even, eventually, to the individual, family, or institution itself.

Problems of self-worth, along with insecurity, seem to be the two single greatest curses of humankind, addressed early on in biblical scripture with the story of Cain and Abel. Most of the destructive behaviors of individuals, families, and institutions revolve around the attempt to preserve and bolster self-image at the expense of others, as well as maintain a position of felt security without regard for one's neighbor.

These destructive behaviors produce anger, and as we have seen, anger is a particularly troublesome emotion for religious institutions. It ruptures the illusion of the perfect family and creates a considerable anxiety on the part of the membership, who worry that the congregational family from whom they derive important nourishment will come apart and die. This is not a far-fetched fantasy because, as we have discussed, congregations do die and dissolve. Unlike biological families, families of faith are, for the most part, not united by blood, and serious disagreement frequently leads to dissolution or at least permanent separation.

Finally, it should be mentioned that interpersonal tension is always exacerbated by environmental stress. Contextual factors having to do with changing demographics, denominational initiatives, and the general tenor of the time contribute to congregational stress. An increase in pressure of this sort weakens congregational resources and the ability to deal effectively with conflict. The following history is called the case of Hope Church because all religious institutions are built on hope, and every behavior of a family of faith, no matter how dysfunctional, is in the service of the hope of self-maintenance.

THE HISTORY OF HOPE CHURCH

The Present Picture

Hope Church presides over the surrounding suburb from its hilltop site in the northeastern part of the United States. Its white clapboard sanctuary is surrounded by a substantial campus that includes administrative offices, an education building, a recreation hall, and housing for two ministers. Hope Church is a program-sized church of about 500 members with a significant history dating back to pre-Revolutionary War times and a budget that approaches half a million dollars. It is part of a "free church" denomination that prides itself in local autonomy and in which hierarchical power flows from the bottom up. However, similar to many other current Protestant families of faith, the congregants of Hope Church come from a great variety of faith perspectives.[1] The majority are, for the most part, white, married, well-educated, upper middle-class folks who are primarily attracted to the landmark church because it is a social center of the town, providing any number of activities, including frequent concerts, AA meetings, a daycare program for young children, and a once-a-year church fair extravaganza that boasts live bands, a fine art auction, and an antique sale. Hope Church's local outreach program currently accounts for 4 percent of its budget.

Hope Church has always liked erudite and well-spoken ministers and prides itself on the preaching ability of its senior staff person. Currently, it is looking for a new minister to fill the position of the one who lately resigned. A couple of years ago, the congregation came up with a new long-range plan because energy and revenues seemed to have been declining for several years, but the plan appears to be having a hard time getting off the ground. In addition, there seems to be a sense in the congregation that community is lacking. In fact, new members don't tend to stick, and old members are leaving or moving away. To counteract this, a small-group program has been initiated and the board has decided that the theme of this year will be a focus on member recruitment. The music program continues to be superb, however, and Hope Church considers it to be the other jewel in its crown. Most of the congregants are certain that everything will be all right as soon as they have found a new senior pastor, who can also head the capital fund drive for the million-dollar renovation and expansion program that the building committee has put together in the interim period. In particular, more parking is needed for the single, though somewhat crowded, service on Sunday.

An Earlier Time: Evidence of Conflict and the Emergence of a Pattern

Let's look back into the archives, however. Hope Church had more humble beginnings. Some 250 years ago, the church was born through the effort of a small group of impoverished but independent farmers. These farmers pulled away from a larger community because of the desire of the fifty founding members for a greater sense of autonomy and control than they experienced in the urban congregation to which they were attached. But from the beginning, the young church had problems, starting with a controversy over the location of the group's first modest house of worship. After several false starts, it was finally constructed, but the structure was never completely finished, as the interior remained unplastered and the balconies accessible only by ladder.

The congregation's first minister, who seemed to become somewhat of an icon in later parish literature, was called on July 4th, 1747 and ordained and installed a month later. He served twenty-six years and then died, suddenly, at an early age. Oddly enough, before calling a new minister, the congregation decided to build a new worship structure a mile or so from the original location. This time the building was completed. Finally, a new pastor was selected, but although he began full-time work immediately, he was not taken under permanent contract until three years later. Irrespective of the fact that he was a published scholar, the second pastor was poorly treated, and when his health began to deteriorate, he was officially dismissed after twenty-one years. The congregation then failed to call a new permanent pastor but relied instead on lay preaching, temporary clergy, and the intermittent services of its dismissed pastor for the next thirty years. Eventually, the congregation decided to build yet a third, more magnificent edifice a few miles further down the road. Although the early historic records of this congregation are amazingly intact, all mention of how this building was designed and in what manner it was financed is strangely missing. Somehow the congregation had decided that in times of stress, be it loss or conflict, it was easier to deflect anxiety by refocusing it on a building project than it was to directly deal with the emotional problem at hand.

A Second Pattern and an Apparent Fear of Clergy

Six years after the new sanctuary was finished, the congregation called a third minister but let him go four years later. Then, for the next 147 years Hope Church retained preachers as sort of "permanent temporary help," without formal contracts. Under this arrangement, ministers were easy to dismiss when the congregation became disaffected with them. In fact, up until 1992, the church's constitution provided that pastors could be removed by a simple majority of persons who appeared at a parish meeting for which only a one-week warning was required. During its lifetime to the present, the congregation ended up employing and dismissing a total of thirty-three pastors, some of whom lasted only two weeks. One stalwart layleader, in reply to the question, "Why are ministers not permanently installed?" was quoted as saying, "If you install them, they're too hard to get rid of." It would seem that Hope Church had, for some reason, a hard time getting along with its ministers in the old days. And, either as a result of the membership's need for control or perhaps an unresolved fear of loss, they never allowed themselves to get too attached. Instead, as we have just seen, when the going got rough, the congregation "cleaned house" by building another building.

Actually, this congregation seemed to raise a major fuss over the issue of roles and rules and who is in charge to do what. Hope Church managed to survive 140 years without a constitution of any sort, and in 1887, when such a document was finally created, the then clergyleader was summarily removed for insisting on bringing it into being. (In the 1992 revision of this document, a preamble was prepared by the then current pastor, which invoked Martin Luther's famous concept of the priesthood of all believers. It aroused a heated stir because the congregants were opposed to "priests and things like that," and the preamble was quickly deleted.)

It appears that conflict, whatever its cause, was pervasive at Hope Church for long periods of time. Even after the construction of the third house of worship, contention apparently continued to run so high that in the late 1800s to mid-1900s, it was not unusual to have only eighteen dedicated parishioners in attendance at Sunday worship, although the building easily sat 250. This caused the congregation to become so poor that it began raising revenues by underwriting first mortgages, a practice that was continued for nearly fifty years.

Hope Church Moves into the Twentieth Century

Sometime in the late 1940s, however, things began to get better, and the congregation began to grow. Grace and goodwill were evident, and by the end of the 1980s, the membership numbered around 350 families and Sunday attendance averaged around 200 persons. Things had been changing in the town, and what had once been a poor but stable rural farming settlement had burgeoned into a transient but prosperous executive bedroom community. The religious fervor of the 1950s and early 1960s had also helped swell the ranks, as had the earnest efforts of several of the parish's most recent, though still beleaguered, clergy.

A Reemergence of Patterns:
Conflict, Control, and Competition

Disaster struck again in the early 1980s, however, when the presiding, and surprisingly long-tenured senior pastor was granted his first sabbatical leave in twenty years, an event that was combined with a growing but unaddressed desire in the parish for better church school leadership. Traditionally, children at Hope Church were better seen than heard, and their education in the Christian faith had, at least in the current pastorate, been left up to laypersons and a series of short-term, assistant ministers who had been hired to help with the growing membership. Sunday school was not the current senior pastor's strong suit, and apparently there continued to be no avenues for the fruitful discussion of alternatives.

Immediately after the senior pastor left for three months overseas, the then current assistant angrily announced that he had accepted a call elsewhere and was departing within weeks. This may have been in response to having been informed that he was to be excluded from the pulpit, even during the absence of the senior pastor. Apparently there was another undiscussable issue—that of the competition between the two ministers. However, there was even yet an additional difficulty, as evidenced in the minutes of the board meetings. Although the senior pastor had managed a significant tenure for the first time since his earliest predecessor, the continuing problem of clergy animosity—perhaps even scapegoating—seemed to have become refocused on the assistant position.

Rallying from a state of shock, an invested group of parishioners began a vigorous search for a highly qualified youth minister and finding exactly what they wanted, employed Reverend Piper in the absence of the senior pastor and at his request, granted him associate status. When the senior pastor returned, the two quickly found that they did not get along, but it was clear to the senior pastor that a decision had been made, and knowing the fate of his earlier colleagues, he decided that he would be foolish to try to change the arrangement.

The next eight years for the two charismatic ministers were difficult, particularly as the associate gathered about himself a strong following in the service of his survival. Reverend Piper also developed a private psychotherapy practice and included many parishioners among his clients, which further confused the pastoral roles. Finally the conflict took its toll, however, and the senior pastor resigned himself to retirement. He had never been formally installed but managed to last thirty years by being careful not to take a public stand on touchy issues and by artfully staying out of power struggles!

The Legacy of Loss and Unresolved Grief and the Beginning of a New Problem

With the departure of the senior pastor, the parish made a wise decision and this time employed an intentional interim minister while it began a search for a new senior minister. After a short year's process, another charismatic preacher was chosen—a choice of consistent importance throughout the church's history. This time he was formally installed. And, perhaps because the parish was feeling bad about the way they had treated their just-resigned pastor, or perhaps because they were afraid they might lose yet another spiritual leader, Reverend Jones' contract was exceedingly generous, in fact, by far the most generous of any ever offered in the history of the parish.

Painful Metaphors and the Repetition of a Problem

As in prior times, when the parish experienced loss or conflict, the congregation once more found itself in the middle of construction. In the interim period and during the first several years of the new pastorate, the membership undertook a major building renovation program, initially replacing the church steeple, laying a new foundation under the sanctuary, and re-siding the historic structure. In some ways, besides being a comfortable deflection from the pain of the recent past, the construction seemed to be a metaphor of the congregation's distress. With renewed effort the parish attempted to point itself toward the heart of God, discover the community on a firmer footing, and put a new face on the congregation to cover what seemed to be its shame and grief.

The former senior pastor, who had family in the area, visited periodically, and requests were made for him to do weddings and funerals. Similar requests were made of the continuing associate pastor, Reverend Piper, who had stayed on. Roles continued to be unclear, and as in the former pastorate, a significant rift developed between Reverend Jones and his associate, along with a similar division of loyalties within the congregation.

These were not the only metaphors, however. Interestingly enough, this time around the parish had chosen a much less conservative minister. His selection may have represented another unresolved separation in the congregation—this time between the conservative old guard—and the upwardly mobile, "modern thinking," younger members of the congregation—reflecting the changing demographics of the community. The liberal Reverend Jones was very much in favor of inclusive language and an open and affirming attitude toward gay and lesbian persons. Perhaps because of a lack of adequate informational, educational, and conversational preparation, his attempts to make the hymnody and the wording of the Sunday service inclusive, coupled with his desire to bless the union of same sex partners, resulted in the resignation of many long-standing congregants, along with the chairperson and several members of the board.

This time, instead of beginning yet another construction project, the membership wisely recognized that it was in trouble. In an attempt to heal itself, the leadership put together a committee of persons to attend to the internal, rather than the external, structure. Another revision of the constitution was undertaken because the congregants had begun to perceive that the present organization was ineffective, the lines of authority were not clear, and its administration did not include enough players. Unfortunately, they did not recognize the impact of the evident, unresolved grief or the lack of conflict-resolution skills. Although only a copy of the most recent constitution could be found, and other archival records for some reason could not be located, the constitution committee worked hard. When the revised document was finished and adopted, Reverend Jones, who intuitively understood the rules of the system, exerted his influence to obtain seats on the board and on all important committees for members loyal to him.

New—and Old—Difficulties

The rift between Reverend Jones and Reverend Piper developed into a chasm, and the congregation decided to terminate the contract of the associate. However, pressure was brought to bear by the contingent of the congregation loyal to Reverend Piper, and still shepherd of the confirmation class, he remained in an attenuated position, much like the historic second pastor of the congregation. Then the parish decided to call a new associate minister.

The new young man was married, unordained, and of a different free church denomination, although this was not unusual to the parish. Timothy found his job definition to be very muddy; the youth group, which had been Reverend Piper's crown, impossible to martial; and the parish engaged in a controversy over whether to have one or two Sunday services, or perhaps enlarge the structure. Although a stunning preacher, he, similar to his prior colleagues, was rarely allowed in the pulpit by Reverend Jones and then mostly on Sundays that were part of poorly attended holiday weekends. Because he was supervised by and reported to Reverend Jones, the governing board remained quite unaware of his problems. Instead, it was overwhelmed with decisions as to how to distribute benevolences and begin a new Stephen's Ministry, while the annual church fair, which produced most of the charitable revenues, began to grow to mythic proportions. Feeling isolated, Timothy struggled through a little more than one year of service. Then suddenly, only two months after his ordination, he anxiously announced to a small but powerful executive committee of the board, newly established as a result of the constitutional revision, that Reverend Jones had been sexually harassing him for an extended period of time. He reported that he had become so fearful that he had begun to clandestinely tape the frequent, uninvited, hours-long, sexualized conversations between himself and his colleague. He had been particularly frightened because the charismatic Reverend Jones sat on the local ordaining body of the denomination, the committee on ministry,[2] and was friendly with the regional executive, who had already twice turned a deaf ear to Timothy's pleas for help.

The Congregational/Denominational Response—
Suppression, Shame, Denial, and Abandonment

The committee, composed mostly of solid supporters of Reverend Jones, was of course taken by surprise and strongly sympathized with the senior pastor, who denied the charges and wept openly about what he maintained was a vicious betrayal. Furthermore, the members of the committee had no knowledge or training regarding the issues of sexual harassment and did not understand the issue of coercive power. They could see no harm in the senior staff person asking the junior pastor to spend weekends alone with him at the senior pastor's secluded vacation home. After all, hadn't Jesus spent time apart with his disciples? Nor were they impressed with the junior pastor's complaint that his superior had repeatedly told him that he just needed a "friend" and had pressed Timothy on some occasions to let him hold the young man's hand. Didn't everybody need a friend, and wasn't it a common thing to hold hands when people prayed? The committee members failed to understand the power dynamic involved in the requests, nor did they think to question the senior pastor as to why he persisted when the associate seemed uncomfortable with the situation. They failed to grasp the difficulty the associate was having in saying "no," due to his subordinate position; they did not comprehend his sense of isolation and helplessness; and for some reason, they did not find his terror regarding the encounters remarkable.

As a result, the young minister felt unprotected and unsupported by the committee's reaction and in a panic, refused to come to work. He was also beginning to feel crazy and to distrust his own judgment, since nobody seemed to feel that anything was wrong. The executive committee chairperson contacted the regional denominational executive who, without informing the local judicatory, quickly sent in a regional staff member to assist in the situation. This "pastoral intervention" effectively avoided any appropriate local judicatory investigative and review process. Upon arrival, the staff representative further minimized the report of the incident, failing to point out the power dynamics involved. He suggested that the two ministers be sent to a counselor "to work it out."

With trepidation, the associate agreed. The church-affiliated counselor, upon hearing the junior pastor's story, excoriated him for taping the conversations and demanded possession of the physical evidence. During the interview it was strongly intimated, by the counselor and Reverend Jones, that it was the associate who had sexualized the situation rather than the senior pastor. Timothy returned from the encounter feeling "dirty," even crazier, and in a state of heightened distress. Not having an advocate, no longer able to trust his experience because it had been challenged by a professional, and now overwhelmed by a sense of acquired shame, Reverend Timothy resigned. A careful letter was drafted to the rest of the parish membership describing the reason for the associate's leaving as "interpersonal problems" between the two colleagues. Reverend Jones was remanded to counseling, quietly paid for by the parish. The associate and his wife were left to fend for themselves. No other governing bodies of the congregation were informed of the details of the situation, and no written records of the event were recorded in the denominational headquarters.

In the aftermath, to prevent problems such as this from happening again, the parish executive committee decided to develop guidelines for staff and clergy evaluation and appointed a three-person personnel committee to deal with delicate matters. Although a significant stir was created in the parish, the story was soon circulated that the problem really had resided with Reverend Timothy, the associate, and now that he was gone, everything was all right. The board requested a report from the executive committee, and assisted by the senior pastor, they embarked on a review of the associate's call and his job performance in the parish.

Shortly thereafter, the church leadership decided to replaster and refinish the inside of the worship space, almost as if it needed another facelift. At this point, because programs seemed to be flagging, the membership also began to develop its new strategic plan. Layleaders were noticing that this, and earlier conflicts, had taken a toll on enrollment, and in spite of the prowess of the new preacher, the census refused to grow. Furthermore, the atmosphere was not improved by the well-meaning efforts of a church historian who had discovered the missing church archives in a cardboard box in the parish office, and whose unflattering chronicles created a considerable controversy.

Shooting the Messenger

Some months later, the congregation called a new associate pastor, Mr. Lamb, also young, unordained, and this time unmarried and not noted for his preaching skills. At this juncture, the parish's student minister, Mr. Thorne, took action. Up until this point, he had remained on the sidelines so as to avoid any possible perceptions of competition on the part of Reverend Jones, since that had been associated with unpleasantness.

Mr. Thorne was an older individual and a credentialed mental health professional, and it was to him, one morning over coffee, that

Reverend Timothy had first disclosed his problem. Mr. Thorne had attempted to intervene earlier, by referring the former associate and his wife to a family therapist experienced in working with issues of sexual abuse and harassment. This was after he had made an earlier unsuccessful attempt to get the denominational representative to do likewise. The referral therapist had confirmed that there was no doubt that harassment had occurred. Mr. Thorne had been struggling with his conscience because he knew that situations such as this have a habit of repeating themselves and that the new candidate could be a certain setup. He finally decided that he was ethically bound to intervene by making the major players in the congregation aware of the problem. In doing so, Mr. Thorne broke the long-standing family rules, "Keep the secret," and "Don't rock the boat."

In response to Mr. Thorne's efforts, Reverend Jones sent several emissaries to keep the student minister in line, including the chairman of the board. When Mr. Thorne asked the chairman if he knew the historic details of the issue, the chairman responded that he didn't want to know. Mr. Thorne was given a gag order by loyal layleaders, although concern was extended to him for his distress. It was also suggested to him by the executive committee, that it might be best if the parish withdrew their sponsorship of Mr. Thorne's ministerial process in order to allow him to leave his painful circumstance.

Mr. Thorne survived the "caring intentions" to terminate his ministerial candidacy and persisted in his attempts to get the secret addressed by seeking out the help of other senior clergy, including the chairperson of the committee on ministry, but to no avail. Months went by and a changing of the guard brought a new regional denominational executive. Mr. Thorne, suffering from continued abuse, threats, and a sense of isolation, and still believing that his church really did not want to condone these matters, approached the denominational leader, who responded by contacting Reverend Jones to see if the allegations were true. Since Reverend Jones denied any wrongdoing, and there was no record of any action in the denominational files, the denominational executive reprimanded Mr. Thorne while standing in solidarity with the senior pastor.

Reverend Jones then confided to his most loyal layleaders his fear, anger, and sense of betrayal by Mr. Thorne. Subsequently, a representative of this group contacted the newly installed successor chairperson of the committee on ministry, communicating their trepidations as to the fitness of Mr. Thorne for ministry, even though the parish board had already submitted their recommendation for his ordination. Reverend Jones reinforced the charge by making it known to his colleagues on the committee that he could not support Mr. Thorne's candidacy.

At this point Mr. Thorne contacted the new chairperson, who moved to protect his candidacy by requiring that any action be the result of a majority decision of the entire parish board. Fortunately for Mr. Thorne, his candidacy survived.

Isolation and Abandonment

Reverend Jones continued his service on the committee on ministry, whose membership was never appraised of the details of the problem. Gradually, the word was passed around both in the congregation and through the clergy grapevine that Mr. Thorne was a "controversial person" and a troublemaker. The seminarian became isolated from fellow congregants and was prevented by Reverend Jones from preaching or contributing to congregational life in any substantive way. Upon graduating from seminary, Mr. Thorne realized that his only hope was to relocate and seek a position in a different state outside the regional denominational jurisdiction, even though his wife had recently established herself as a partner in a local business firm.

The Aftermath: Symbolic Issues, Conflict, Disconnection, Paralysis, and Deflection

Meanwhile, the new associate pastor was not having an easy time. Although he was now ordained and working hard, the youth program was still floundering, and congregants were beginning to gossip and disapprove of Reverend Lamb's recent romantic relationship. In fact, things got so hot that another member of the board resigned, along with several old-time members of the congregation. Perhaps symbolically, sex, sexuality, and gender issues continued to be a testy topic amongst the membership.

The board became concerned that the parish was becoming disconnected, as the informal social group structure that had been put in place by the former senior pastor had almost vanished. The historic Women's League, which had raised much of the parish revenue in previous years and served as a connecting point with other parishes, had collapsed. The new members, at least those who stuck, were also complaining about the uncongenial after-service coffee hour, and old members were complaining about the lack of pastoral visitation. The number of committees had been vastly increased by the new constitution, and in order to increase participation, even more recent adjustments had made it impossible for a congregant to serve on more than one committee. However, fewer and fewer people were showing up to undertake the tasks at hand, and none of the newly visioned programs seemed to be getting off the ground.

So, a lay-caretaking program was designed, and committee meetings were moved to a single weekday evening with a group worship service preceding it. A new phone system was installed, and work was begun on a complete refurbishing of the parish hall kitchen. It was almost as if, in the unconscious mind of the parish, it was hoped that, as in the warm fuzzy ads for Ma Bell, new phone lines would connect them. Moreover, the kitchen project, while it once again provided a needed distraction, perhaps was conceived as an unconscious and symbolic way to restore the emotional nurturance that was lacking.

However, by this time, Reverend Jones had finished six years of service and requested his sabbatical. Two months into his leave he returned and announced that he had accepted a call to another, much larger, parish unaffiliated with the denomination. The congregation was in shock, but its layleadership rallied almost immediately. Even though pledges had been in a decline for the last several years and attendance was down, the board announced a million-dollar building plan, which included an enlargement of the sanctuary. Although the funding was in question work would begin immediately on the renovation of the Christian education building.

AN ANALYSIS OF BEHAVIORAL PATTERNS

Of course, the first thing that we can learn from the story of Hope church is that it is a bad idea to allow a former assistant or associate pastor to stay in place after the calling of a new senior minister. Issues of competition and loyalty almost inevitably ensue, and the continued tenure of a former minister makes it very difficult for the new pastor to become "part of the family." This, of course, is why, in many denominations, it is considered unethical for a contractually terminated spiritual leader, even if he or she is retired, to hang around his or her former parish.

The worst scenario, however, is when a congregation thinks it can save money by not using the services of an intentional interim. Frequently in these cases, the assistant or associate is allowed to assume the "acting, head of staff" role, and then upon calling a new senior pastor, he or she is thanked for a job well done by demoting him or her back to junior staff status. This is parallel to the married couple, usually with a male child, who obtains a divorce, with the mother retaining sole custody. The mother (or the church) begins to rely on the child (the associate) for emotional and sometimes even physical support. Actually, they become symbolically "married." Then, when the mother finds a suitable adult partner (the new senior pastor) and decides to recouple, the "parentified" child is demoted back to kid status by the new pair. Needless to say, he or she hates this and causes all sorts of trouble. If he or she has younger siblings, he may martial their loyalty against the "interloper" and really cause a problem. Sometimes, in a situation like this, the new husband can never really get into or become part of the system, and the second marriage, or pastorate, also falls apart.

In the case of Hope Church, however, much more is going on. Historic and continuing patterns symptomatic of poor conflict-resolution resources, a distrust of clergy, unresolved grief, competition, a need for control, along with maneuvers by small power groups, shame, and secrecy are present. The sexual misconduct may actually be an old issue, now symbolically reenacted. Archival evidence pointed to at least one possible incident, and reports from two members of the congregation indicated that something of the sort occurred between a more recent senior pastor and a junior staff member, who also was caused to leave under a shroud of closely held secrecy.

Conflict, Control, and a Distrust of Clergy

The hallmarks of underground power struggles at Hope Church are easily seen in the earliest controversies over the location of the sanctuary. Pervasive conflict is evidenced in the impoverished attendance of many years duration, leading to severe financial difficulties, and is memorialized in an archival sermon delivered at the church's 100th anniversary by the unhappy pastor of that era, who attempted to cause the congregation to look at itself and address the problem. In more recent times, unresolved conflict is evidenced by the calling of the new associate in the temporary absence of the senior pastor. For most of its history, the term of a pastor was tenuous at Hope Church, aided by a congregational determination not to install clergy or provide them with a contract, along with the constitutional provision that allowed ministers to be easily dismissed. The most notable incident of this sort was the struggle over the first constitution, a battle of control that finally ended up in the courts, with the preacher suing the parish. The early church fathers were clear in their desire to keep the visible rules and the nature of roles obscure, as well as keep the power in the hands of a few leaders with lifetime terms of office. Exactly the cause of clergy mistrust in the early history of the church is not clear, but certainly ministers had a hard time "getting married" to Hope Church.

Grief

Although it may not seem initially evident, Hope Church also has a hard time saying "good-bye." In the recent past, the tendency to hang on to and overidealize the former long-term senior pastor, as well as complaints about the lack of pastoral visitation, probably have to do with issues of unresolved grief that this immobilized parish is unable to process. An inability of this congregation to let go of its leaders in a healthy way is further substantiated by the congregation's difficulty in terminating the employment of its first associate pastor, Reverend Piper, as well as its most recent announcement that when a new senior pastor is called, the current associate, Reverend Lamb, will stay on.[3] This is actually the flip side of the coin that had been previously expressed by Hope Church's summary dismissal of so many of its spiritual leaders.

It is possible that this problem began with the untimely death of the congregation's first pastor, as the parish certainly seemed ambivalent about its second. Tellingly, history tells us that the first and second ministers were family relatives and preached a similar message, a significant signal of the unresolved grief of at least part of the congregation! Not surprisingly, the second pastor was unable to fill his predecessor's shoes, or make the congregation happy, as evidenced by his complaints of mistreatment rendered in a posthumously delivered sermon.

It is never possible to replace a person or a relationship because every human being is unique, with a unique history, and try as we might, we can never replicate what we had. Our replacements always fall short of the measure, and unfortunately, we often have a tendency to blame these persons for not living up to the task. Indeed, the problem with saying "hello" to a person or a pastor is that since we are finite beings, every "hello" implies a "good-bye." And parting with a beloved significant other is painful for all of us. Sometimes, when the pain is too terrible, we decide never to do it again. So we unconsciously avoid connecting or forming a serious relationship with someone to whom we might get attached. This may be part of what went on, and still goes on, at Hope Church.

Scapegoating

Hope Church is also prone to a lot of scapegoating. Whether it blames its unhappiness and unacknowledged sense of loss on "replacement" pastors, or transfers its resentment to associate pastors, the real issues at hand never get addressed. When conflict arises, the congregation looks around to find an individual to fault, rather than recognizing that it is the entire system that needs to be healed.

Shame

There are a lot of indications, in spite of its shiny face, that Hope Church is ashamed of itself. For most of its history the congregation treated its ministers, and apparently many of their fellow parishioners, badly. Frequently, we treat persons badly because this is a projection of the way we feel about ourselves. Instead of loving our neighbor as ourselves, we disrespect our neighbor because we are disrespectful of ourselves. As was mentioned earlier, the suddenly very generous contract provided to the first-time-in-a-long-time installed Reverend Jones, may also be a symptom of shame and the need to make up for past trespasses. The subsequent decision of the board not to publish his further salary increases, whatever the rationalization, would also lead one's thinking in this direction. The constant "cleaning house" in the way of rebuilding, replastering, and repainting may, besides being a convenient distraction from the pain of conflict, also be an unconscious attempt at covering or cleaning away the shame. This is sort of like Lady Macbeth's line, "Out, damned spot! out, I say!"[4] Of course, the cause of the shame may come from several sources.

The Footprints of a Secret

Hope Church is also very much involved in secret-keeping. The footprints of secrecy, a corollary of power problems, as we saw in Chapter 6, also run through the history of this community. To this end, let us look through the lens of Chilton Knudson's constructs.[5] Particularly noticeable are the *distraction and smoke-screen patterns*. These are easily seen early in the first constitutional fight, particularly when one reads the transcript of the court case that oddly enough the parish retained in its archival files. Apparently there was some substantial confusion or obfuscation regarding *responsibility and lines of authority*, which was maintained by not having a formal document. The *role confusion* between the two associates, Timothy and the Reverend Piper is another part of this pattern, as is the earlier role confusion between Reverend Piper and Reverend Jones, which precipitated another constitutional revision. All in all, in its attempt to eliminate confusion, this congregation, in the period between 1897 and 1992, revised and significantly amended its constitution six times.

The *tendency to focus on trivial and routine matters*, such as benevolences, including the church fair and the number of services, is another distraction pattern, as are *secret or rump meetings of powerful parties*, as symbolized by the group that superintended the calling of the associate during the senior pastor's sabbatical. A fourth distraction pattern, *inadequate systems of communication*, is represented by the poor supervisory and reporting configuration that helped maintain the secret of abuse between Reverend Jones and Reverend Timothy. It is also seen in the feelings of disconnectedness that led to the shepherding program and the felt organizational ineffectiveness that led to the constitutional revisions. Furthermore, part of Timothy's vulnerability resulted in his feelings of isolation from parish members, since little attempt had been made to integrate him and his wife into the community, perhaps as a result of loyalties to Reverend Piper. The fact that he came from a different denomination further intensified the problem.

Yet other distraction and smoke-screen patterns include *weak or absent processes for clergy and staff evaluation*, as evidenced by the need to develop them as well as the Teflon aura around Reverend Jones; *an absence as to a consensus regarding mission*, as indicated by the felt need to develop a visioning process and long-range plan; and *a pattern of overactivity with no follow-through*, which is most notably observed in all the new programs that were not happening. And then of course, there was the historic major distraction of building and refurbishing that seemed to be the community's first line of defense.

The second group of patterns that can be observed in this congregation are those behaviors that purpose *to keep the secret*. It would seem that perhaps there had been at least several secrets during the history of this parish. This is evidenced by the *absence of files and meeting minutes* of the construction of the current worship structure, as well as the process of the calling of the charismatic first associate, the dismissal of a whole string of other assistants, and of other matters that came before the board, particularly with regard to clergy employees. Included here might also be the mysterious absence, followed by the later discovery, of the archival materials in the church office, including the lost constitutions. In fact, Hope Church was so averse to keeping records that it did not record the marriages, funerals, and in more recent times, even baptisms, of its congregants! Other protective phenomena, such as the *disappearance of vital programs,* may be evidenced by the difficulties with the youth program, the disappearance of the Women's League, and the earlier disappearance of a somewhat controversial social action committee. A *reluctance to remember past events* is evidenced by the stir caused by the church historian and the deafness encountered by the pained pastor that preached the one-hundredth-year sermon. Speaking eloquently of repeating patterns, this sermon was, oddly enough, unearthed and published fifty years later, and copies were found in the archives by the meddling historian. *Subtle or overt discrediting of persons who have left the church* occurred with the released associate minister, Reverend Timothy, as did the *circula-*

tion of inaccurate stories about the leader's departure. In the case
of the student minister, Mr. Thorne, this discrediting was not so
subtle. Certainly, in this case, his gag order, and the unwillingness
of the board chairperson to avail himself of accurate and complete
information, was *a rule or taboo against discussing the event* of the
associate's departure. There was also a significant rule against discussing what was probably a similar occurrence in a prior pastorate.
The demise of the parish social groups may have been simply an
attrition caused by demographics, or it may at least partially have
been related to the need to *create isolation and disconnectedness in
order to prevent the spread of secret knowledge.* The problems with
the coffee hour may also be a reflection of the community rule
proscribing the discussion of the secret or secrets with the resultant
disconnectedness.

The third group of behaviors, *avenues for the discharge of rage
and anger,* is represented by the *scapegoating* of the most recent
associate minister, Reverend Lamb, as well as the student minister,
Mr. Thorne. Rage and the lack of conflict-resolution skills abound,
but are most recently evident in the *departures of membership,*
including layleadership. A second pattern, *voting with the pocket-
book or the withholding of contributions,* is evidenced in the decline
in church revenues, as well as the earlier financial distress that
caused the congregation to underwrite first mortgages. The *selection of "targets"* is a long-time pattern of this parish, represented by
its historic anticlericalism and clergy-killer behavior. *Blaming the
victim* can be observed with respect to the lack of support and the
stories circulated regarding the terminated associate, Reverend
Timothy. *Stoning the messenger* is evidenced by the response of the
congregation, certain members of the board, and other senior clergy
to the actions of the student minister. The lack of energy for program participation and committee attendance is indicative of *congregational depression.* The early narratives of Hope Church are
full of manipulation and power struggles, which continue to resur-
face and can be observed between layleaders and the clergy;
between the former senior pastor, his assistants, and the first
associate minister, Reverend Piper; between Reverend Jones and all
three associate ministers; and between Reverend Jones and the student minister, Mr. Thorne. Finally, *"murder" in the guise of caring*

can be seen in the action taken against the student minister by the congregation that sought to care for him by relieving him of his ordination process.

The fourth group of secret and conflict-related behaviors, *symbolic expressions*, is most stunningly represented by the congregation's historic pattern of "cleaning house" by constructing or refurbishing sanctuaries *between* pastorates. In fact, in this parish, all anxiety, including that generated by unresolved grief, seems to be dealt with by building and renovating the physical plant, even when it makes no economic sense. Even the need for nurturance and connectedness is responded to by redoing the parish kitchen, and an attempt to correct the lack of adequate communication is done by installing a new phone system. A further symbolic behavior, *preoccupation with sexual matters,* may be observed in the hot debate over the use of inclusive language and the blessing of gay relationships, as well as the controversy concerning the new associate's intimate other. It would again seem, from the past history of the parish and the decided anticlericalism, that Reverend Jones' alleged sexual misconduct was not the first of such occurrences, and as has been mentioned, it is quite possible that this was a *symbolic reenactment* of what may have been several earlier insults.

The final group of behaviors characteristic of a congregation with a secret are those that reflect *feelings of violation and shame.* Although the recent senior pastor, Reverend Jones, was *hypervigilant, suspicious, and distrustful* and the congregants have been, for the most part, *passive* or even paralyzed, the roles have swapped back and forth. The greater body historically had allowed a small number of powerful members to run the show, even when it came to engaging in untimely building projects. A laissez-faire policy seemed to apply to the evaluation of Reverend Jones, as nobody was able to take him on, even when his behavior was questionable. In fact, the congregation had a rule that nothing bad was to be said about Reverend Jones, even if he was not living up to expectations. This was an odd, 180-degree reversal of the previous pattern of serious judgmentalism with respect to clergy. As we saw earlier, his handsome compensation package seemed to be an attempt to correct for the impoverished and even punitive way the congregation had managed its previous spiritual leaders. Currently, parishioners who become disillusioned simply withdraw from the congregation and fade away. Furthermore, *little attempt is made to encourage or involve newcomers*, certainly not at the coffee hour, or by expanding the one crowded service to two, or even enlarging the parking lot. Interestingly enough, the student minister was told by one layleader that he should be ashamed of having his sponsorship nearly terminated. Finally, besides physical "whitewash," congregational dis-ease and the need to purify itself was treated by tweaking the programming, launching a "spiritual values," educational campaign, and attempting to put a renewed emphasis on Bible study.

The Future of Hope Church

Hope Church has a real problem. It has valiantly tried to heal itself in a variety of ways, many of which have been partially successful, but none of which have cut to the core of the issue. Not healed from the inside out, the wounds continue to fester. With respect to the clergy misconduct, it just happened that sexual misconduct had occurred at the regional denominational level among ordained administrative staff some years earlier. The incident had been quietly dealt with by asking the offending executive to resign without making the truth public. Pastor Jones, it turned out, was to be protected not only by his peers and the then-current denominational executive, but also by the successor executive. This individual, interestingly enough, took the initiative at an annual denominational meeting to honor his impeached predecessor, again without disclosing the reason for the leader's "retirement."

In his letter to Mr. Thorne, reprimanding him for disclosing the allegation of misconduct between the senior pastor and Reverend Timothy, the successor executive wrote the following:

> The matter was properly aired and resolved between the two ministers and key layleaders from the congregation . . . I have been advised by the chair [of the Committee on Ministry] that your responses to the committee have also been unsatisfactory and that there are real questions about your fitness and preparedness for ministry . . . in recent years the [regional denomination] has dealt forthrightly with cases of clergy misconduct. Guidelines are in place and in good working order and the process is above reproach.

Actually, this particular region of the denomination did not adopt *any* guidelines for clergy sexual misconduct until two years after the incident at Hope Church first occurred. And that decision was not binding upon the local judicatory, which did not finally ratify the guidelines until an additional two years down the line. Moreover, Mr. Thorne had not been asked to meet with or respond to the committee on ministry since the time he had entered the process four years previously. This disconnection between the student and the players in his ministerial process may not have been a conscious interruption of communication, but it was at least an unconscious avoidance in the service of preventing dissemination of knowledge of the secret. The chair of the committee on ministry did apologize to Mr. Thorne, however, for the successor executive's apparent misunderstanding of her communication with him. Perhaps the executive had confused the opinion of the committee on ministry with the opinion of one of its constituents, Reverend Jones.

After Pastor Jones' resignation and departure for his new parish, Hope Church began what, for it, was a groundbreaking effort at recuperating. Although many older congregants believed that everything would be solved if only a new senior pastor were quickly found, Hope Church took a significant step outside its defensive structure and hired a consultant. Unfortunately, in this case, the corporate dynamics were too seductive, and the well-meaning consultant, who was himself a clergyperson, became quickly co-opted by the system into maintaining the secret. He was immediately inducted into a silent, protective stance by the small administrative committee that had dealt with the problem between Reverend Jones and his associate. He was persuaded not to work with the greater body of the board, that broad-based data collection was not necessary, nor was a public report, and that the only difficulties which needed addressing were the theological and communication problems that existed with respect to the conservative versus liberal views on inclusive language.

Like the patient who presents for psychotherapy, hoping not for change but to become more proficient at being neurotic, Hope Church hopes for a greater sense of connectedness and better communication patterns, so long as it does not have to address the reasons for their absence. Sadly enough, the consultant was not sufficiently savvy. In the end, Hope Church may hope in vain.

Chapter 10

Reowning Responsibility

Most of us think of responsibilities as those things that we are supposed to do—our obligations, those tasks that we have taken on, the burdens that we carry in work, family, and community. We are "responsible" employees and get to work on time; we are "responsible" parents and provide for our children; we are "responsible" citizens and go to the polls on election day. There is another form of responsibility however, one that has a lighter yoke but heavier consequences. Here, in the context of the family of faith, we need to look at personal responsibility, as well as corporate responsibility in the light of ethics and ethical systems. And we need to look at how we can reown that responsibility through the use of consultants, preventative maintenance, the creation of boundaries, and pro-active clergy training.

PERSONAL RESPONSIBILITY

Personal responsibility is responsibility to oneself. Sometimes it is called existential responsibility. It is not about performing tasks but more about the way one is in the world. It is not about doing but rather about being. It is about personal honesty, being able to study oneself in a glass clearly. And it is about ethical behavior, being able and resolved to act according to one's conscience, no matter what the personal cost. Personal responsibility is about becoming conscious and taking ownership of one's traits, behaviors, and motivations and then taking an active, rather than a passive role with respect to the environment, be that job, family, community, or community of faith. Personal responsibility is a conscious "yes" and a conscious "no," rather than simply letting things happen, burying one's head in the sand, or looking the other way. Personal responsibility is about heal-ing the self so that one can love one's neighbors.

ETHICAL BEHAVIOR AND ETHICAL SYSTEMS

Now let us look at the concept of ethical behavior. Ethics is the study of moral issues: good/evil, right/wrong, responsive/irrespon-sive, and liberating/oppressing. None of these examples are really dichotomies, but continuums. There are lesser and greater evils and lesser or greater freedoms. Ethical behavior is action taken along these continuums.

In addition, there are ethical systems, or particular methods of determining what is good, right, responsive, and even liberating. These may be classed as deontological, teleological, and responsive. A *deontological ethic* asks, "What is the law?" and emphasizes an adherence to abstract principles using deductive reasoning. A *teleo-logical ethic* asks, " What is the goal?" and holds the end as ulti-mately more important than the means. An *ethic of responsibility*[1] asks, "What is happening?" and then, "What is the fitting response to what is happening?" An ethic of responsibility takes into account who is involved, why the action occurred in the circumstance of the particular community, and finally, what is the most fitting response to that action in the context of a continuing society.

AN ETHIC OF RESPONSIBILITY

The word responsibility comes from the Latin root, *spondere*, mean-ing "to pledge" or "to promise." Therefore to respond is "to promise in return" or "to reply." Responsibility is the state of response or the capacity to respond. An ethic of responsibility answers persons in the context of their situations. It is an interactive process *that implies accountability* in which an action meets a previous action and antici-pates a reply. Each action looks forward as well as backward and is a part of a total conversation that has meaning as a whole.

If we compare the three ethical systems, we would see that a deontological ethic might say "Stealing is bad" and would then punish the thief. A teleological ethic would say "The goal is a crimeless society" and would then punish the thief. But an ethic of responsibility would say "Who is the thief? Taking into account the context of the community [including power imbalances], why did he or she steal?" And finally, "If we are to have a better society for *all* parties concerned, what is the best course of action?"

Personal responsibility is necessary to the employment of an ethic of responsibility. This is because the agent who is acted upon, in this case the one who was robbed, must be able to honestly look at the situation, including his or her own power position and agendas. If the thief was starving and stole for food, and the "victim" was wealthy and of a majority class whose societal rules imprisoned the thief in poverty, an ethic of responsibility would require a different answer. The reason we like the story of Robin Hood is that we intuitively understand that he and his band of men, though "robbers," by enacting this ethic sought to bring about social justice in an oppressive time.

CORPORATE RESPONSIBILITY

Corporate responsibility is the responsibility of the community toward one another and the environment. The concept of ethical community, which was spoken about earlier in this chapter, derives from the idea that a true community, by its very nature, strives to support, sustain, and enable every member to develop to his or her greatest potential in the context of a continuing society. Ethical community implies that the membership of the group, as a whole, strives to become conscious of its actions and agendas, to the end that they should not cause harm to any individual but instead contribute to a greater life for all concerned.

Historically, the prophetic vision of religious communities of the Judeo-Christian heritage has been one of ethical community of this sort. Unfortunately, however, our religious institutions have had a tendency to adhere to deontological and teleological ethical systems, perhaps because they are simpler and less messy. With respect to the first, it is important to realize that relying on a rule to make one's decision effectively gives away the responsibility to the rule maker, or even to the abstract principle itself. If, for instance, we say "homosexuality is bad," then we do not have to address the pain, suffering, isolation, and social injustice in our community that accompanies homophobia. Or, if we say "adultery is bad," we do not have to address the power dynamics inherent in clergy sexual misconduct when it involves a married parishioner, and instead we can scapegoat the victim.

Likewise, in the case of the teleological ethic, relying on a goal on which to make one's decision gives license to all sorts of atrocities in the name of that which is holy. If our goal is to preserve orthodoxy, then the tortures of the Inquisition make sense, as the goal of doctrinal purity is more important than the means by which it was attained. And, if our goal is to preserve our community of faith by avoiding conflict, or retain our spiritual leader because of his preaching ability, then ignoring or covering up clergy misconduct also makes sense.

However, if religion is about compassion, and it appears that all great religions come together at that place, it would seem more fitting if communities of faith adopted instead an ethic of responsibility, where we are accountable not only to the law, to rules, and our goals, but also to victims and the disenfranchised. It is here that the widow and the stranger are cared for, and one's "sins" are seen in the same light as the greater sins of the community. It is here that the messenger is received and not stoned. It is here that we can find compassion, help, and healing for not only the victim(s) of clergy misconduct but also for the perpetrator and the community.

In more traditional terms, an ethic of responsibility is about confession. It is about *all* parties owning their misdeeds and ugly agendas. This must then be followed by taking action to remedy any damage caused—an action called penitence. Confession and penitence must precede reconciliation, which is then the coming to wholeness of the entire community. Some would see this whole process as the work of God through grace. Since the early history of the peoples of the book, the prophets have cried out concerning social justice. When we fail to employ an ethic of responsibility, we stop hearing their voices.

THE ROLE OF CONSULTANTS
IN REOWNING RESPONSIBILITY

The process of reowning responsibility for the hurtful behavior patterns, which we have been discussing in the last several chapters, can be facilitated in many ways. Most often, some sort of consultant is useful in this journey. We will not deal in-depth with this process here, as there is already significant literature in the marketplace.[2] However, a short synopsis of what this looks like is useful.

Data Collection and the Impartial Observer

The "confession" stage of healing and reconciliation always begins with gathering data about what happened and how. This needs to be done in an objective way, by persons who are conscious of their own feelings and agendas and honest about how they impact on the process. Consultants are useful when dealing with all sorts of institutional distress, including congregational development difficulties, financial dilemmas, values disputes, and personnel problems. In many, if not most cases of clergy misconduct, it is useful to employ a consultant who is outside the particular religious system, and who has no disciplinary authority. However, as was demonstrated in the case of Hope Church, the power of family rules within the system, and the subtle coercive forces used to support them, cannot be over-emphasized. Consultants frequently fail because in some way they are co-opted by the systemic rule of secrecy. When the investigator is part of the system, as in the case of an intervening judicatory administrator, it is very difficult to draw a boundary between what is best for all parties involved, versus the particular needs of the person(s) collecting and analyzing the data. Furthermore, clergy, denominational executives, and congregations are so uncomfortable with the issue of clergy sexual misconduct that, if the situation appears quiet on the surface, they are all too ready to dismiss the notion that any enduring damage has been done to the congregation. Less than full disclosure always leads to a festering wound that, if not eventually addressed, eats at the system like a cancer. Incestuous systems do not heal themselves of their own accord.

As we have discussed, most religious institutions are composed of interlocking systems of individual communities and larger regional administrative bodies. Similar to the yeast in dough, they are part of one another and to a greater or lesser degree, depending upon the particular polity, cannot function entirely separately. A majority of denominations have some form of internal review and disciplinary process, perhaps a crisis response team, and a cadre of internal congregational consultants. Interveners or consultants who are also denominational officials at various levels, or consultants hired by a judicatory for the specific purpose of removing a spiritual leader, are part of the system and influenced by it. In some cases, they may even have dual roles, that of data gathering and counseling, as well as that of discipline. This makes the working contract between the consultant and the community of faith very fuzzy, as it is impossible to be an advocate and a judge at the same time. It is important to remember that in the case of alleged clergy misconduct, dual relationships of this sort provide the opportunity for significant betrayal of either the congregant, the community, or the clergyperson.

In addition, an ordained, judicatory executive is also subject to loyalty needs—a fact that has been amply born out by the effects of the "old boy" network that has historically sought to protect clergy brethren and the institutional reputation, rather than care for victims and heal communities. Likewise, a judicatory executive or administrative council may also have a strong need to "disappear" a clergyperson who they perceive to be a problem, in order to save face or restore an otherwise damaged denominational image.

Reporting

After broad-based interviewing by a *neutral* or impartial observer has yielded adequate data about what happened and how, along with the recognition of the significant resources of the community, the family of faith needs to be informed. After extensive information has been gathered and analyzed, the entire community should be provided with both a written and oral report. This is delivered in the context of a public gathering of the body, the purpose of which is to allow the membership to correct any misconceptions that the consultant might have, as well as bring to light the nature of the conflictual issues—*including any secrets*. This allows the membership to learn, to react, and to begin to process the contents of the report in the context of visible companionship, thereby providing a opportunity to build community at a crucial moment. The consultant then contracts with the guiding body of the congregation, such as the board, the council, the vestry, or the session, to work on those issues that the congregation feels are most important. When clergy misconduct is one of the issues, the necessary denominational authorities are also contacted, so that appropriate procedures may be initiated. Disclosure is not made without provisions being in place for an intentional, supportive healing process.

The Community Makes Its Own Choices

A consultant does not wave a magic wand but collects data and then supports and guides the congregation, enabling the membership to access, strengthen, and use its resources in the healing process. A consultant does not make the community's choices for it but only provides awarenesses and additional resources. As we have already seen in the case of Hope Church, the consultant can only travel with a congregation the distance that it wishes to go on its journey toward wholeness. Just as Jesus of Nazareth said, "Your faith [has made you well]," so a congregation may be healed according to the extent of its faith and its desire (Mt9:22; Mk5:34, 1o:52; Lk8:48, 17:19).

In the Christian scriptures, one of the most difficult teachings of Jesus of Nazareth, and one frequently passed over in the Lectionary readings, is Mt 10:34-38 (RSV):

> Do not think that I have come to bring peace on earth; I have not come to bring peace, but a sword. For I have come to set a man against his father, and a daughter against her mother, and a daughter-in-law against her mother-in-law; and a man's foes will be those of his own household. He who loves father or mother more than me is not worthy of me; and he who loves son or daughter more than me is not worthy of me; and he who does not take his cross and follow me is not worthy of me.

Here Jesus seems to be referring to, and in some cases, even quoting the prophet Micah, a younger contemporary of Isaiah, who is crying to his people, the Israelites, about the social injustice of his time and culture (Micah 7:6-7). Micah, Amos, Hosea, and Isaiah were fierce champions of social justice and God's judgment, as well as being prophets of the promise of divine forgiveness and the hope of future restoration. Jesus puts a more immediate twist on this message, however, indicating that even the present upheaval *that he will create* is not necessarily evil or to be seen as punishment, but instead is requisite to healing.

Resolving congregational conflict, especially when there has been scapegoating, family secrets, and clergy misconduct, initially causes a crisis—the very crisis that the congregation has been trying to avoid. But, just as a surgeon must use a scalpel to make the incision that will enable the eventual healing of the patient, the consultant must make an incisive intervention in the form of truth-telling in order for the congregation to become whole. The crisis may initially be a crisis of dissension and of the fear of fracture—of mother against daughter and son against father—as each member receives the information through the lens of his or her worldview and current faith perspective. God's call then becomes the conversation and the struggle that must ensue as the family of faith begins, in a supportive atmosphere, to digest the information and take a new look at itself.

Disclosures of Clergy Sexual Misconduct

In particular, disclosures of clergy misconduct are experiences of loss—the loss of the perfect family and the loss of the perfect leader/parent/god. The first task of healing involves the processing of the various stages of grieving:[3] shock, denial, bargaining, anger, and finally, the sense of loss itself. These stages are not a linear occurrence. They may present in the form of a spiral with several sequential manifestations of each feature.

Shock is the initial "numb" stage during which the congregation hears the news but cannot really react, except in some fairly meaningless task-oriented activity, similar to picking out a casket in a funeral home. It is even common for congregations at this point to tell consultants that they are "okay" and can manage alone. Generally, they are not okay.

Denial, the next feature of the grief process, is the state of disbelief that such a thing could happen or be true. Denial is apparent when a congregation wants to proceed with business as usual even when it is clear that there is a problem. When denial wears thin, the bargaining stage often begins to surface. Bargaining is the attempt to substitute one cost for another. One possible manifestation of bargaining is the expressed desire to allow the perpetrator to stay on, if only he or she participates in therapy, which the parish will pay for.

Anger is the point at which the clergyperson finally falls from his or her pedestal. The anger may also be redirected at the spouse for not being sufficiently supportive of the clergyperson, or at the victim for being "seductive" and therefore responsible for the loss. Congregants may also blame themselves for not taking adequate care of their spiritual leader, with the resultant feelings of shame.

The felt sense of loss is the last stage of the grieving process. In addition to the loss of an illusion is the emptiness and perhaps, the sense of leaderlessness left by the departure of a teacher, counselor, spiritual guide, administrator and maybe friend. Loss and grief are like a gaping hole in the belly through which blows the winter wind. Yet it is out of this crisis that re-creation begins.

Mending Broken Behavior Patterns

A second, very important piece of work that needs to be done when there has been clergy misconduct is an examination of the structure and behavioral patterns of the congregation that enabled the problem to evolve. Questions that need to be asked are the following: "Have there been other such occurrences?"; "What sort of spiritual leaders does this congregation have a tendency to search for? Does it look for spectacular, charismatic preachers who have a narcissistic personality that makes them vulnerable to being abusive?"; "What is the structure of this congregation? Is it authoritarian? Who has the power, and how is it distributed? Are roles and boundaries fuzzy or clearly drawn? How are the staff, including clergy, evaluated?"; "What are the family messages of this congregation? Is it secretive? What are the communication patterns of this congregation?"; " How does this congregation manage conflict? How is anger expressed?"; "What is the quality of this congregation's relationship with the larger denomination?"; and finally, "How does this congregation feel about itself?" When the answers to these questions indicate a vulnerability on the part of the community of faith for a repeat occurrence, these issues need to be addressed.

Ethical Behavior for Consultants

Finally, something should be said about ethical behavior with respect to consultants themselves. Unfortunately, as in the case of Hope Church, consultants can also be destructive. Consultants enable healing by virtue of their position as a *neutral*. Whenever this role is violated because the professional has failed to keep adequate boundaries between his or her task and his or her own fears and biases, the outcome can be extraordinarily damaging. In the case of situations involving clergy misconduct, inadequately trained, unethical, or personally unaware consultants can revictimize the primary and secondary victims by denying their reality and leaving them open to further scapegoating and even vicious assault.

Ordained persons who are congregational conflict-resolution consultants need to separate themselves from their tendency to champion clergy perpetrators. At its most innocuous, such behavior is in the service of an unconscious desire on the part of the consultant for self-protection. At its worst, it is simple collusion. Consultants who conceal or fail to reveal important, documented data, particularly in the case of clergy sexual misconduct, are themselves guilty of the worst form of abuse and abandonment of primary and secondary victims, in addition to serious ethical misconduct. Consultants who lay blame for congregational craziness at the feet of beleaguered "afterpastors," clergy who follow the pastorate of an abuser, become destructive rather than healing. Such action simply serves to justify the injustice done to these secondary victims. Unfortunately, behavior of this sort is not unheard of, and part of reowning responsibility is the establishment of adequate ethical guidelines for consultants, including supervision, peer-review processes, and disciplinary procedures.

Finally, the organizational development model, long used for religious institution consultation, is simply not fitted to instances where clergy sexual misconduct is suspected. Unlike the family systems model, which has recently come into use by a growing number of professionals in this field, the organizational development model is not equipped with a framework for understanding and dealing with the phenomenon of sexual abuse and harassment by spiritual leaders. When hiring a consultant, it is important to inquire into his or her credentials, experience, *and training*, particularly with respect to family systems, and when possible obtain references from congregations that have used this person to deal with similar issues. Currently, the only national organization that credentials conflict-resolution consultants is the Society for Professionals in Dispute Resolution (SPIDR), and that organization, which mostly concerns itself with labor disputes, does not require systems training.

REOWNING RESPONSIBILITY THROUGH PREVENTATIVE MAINTENANCE

The concept of preventative maintenance is not a common one for congregations. Unfortunately, religious institutions most often operate with a "don't fix it if it ain't broke" attitude. This is usually because of the fence of protection and denial that often surrounds communities of faith, as they try to maintain the illusion of the perfect family that will never fall apart.

Early-maintenance consultation is a way to avoid crisis and serious congregational wounding. In this format, best used in a pastorate three to five years old, a data-gathering process facilitates the identification of strengths and any possible problems, so that weaknesses may be remedied and strengths can be enabled to realize their full potential. This sort of consultation serves as an affirmation to the spiritual leadership and to the community of a job well done and develops a reservoir of resources for negotiating the inevitable rocky places in the road.

Besides enabling a congregation to celebrate its ministry and its competencies, a consultation of this sort might discover unresolved grief over the leaving of a previous beloved pastor that, left unattended, might result in the scapegoating of the present clergy once the honeymoon was over. If there is need, consultants might suggest the usefulness of a Stephens's Ministry, a well-developed therapist referral list, or even an in-house counseling center using trained mental health workers instead of extended one-on-one counseling with the pastors. Or a consultant might suggest the provision of the opportunity for supervision of clergy doing significant counseling. An early-maintenance consultation might identify family messages that need to be made conscious and talked about. It might identify potentially problematic communication patterns and suggest and provide additional skill training. It might suggest a different distribution of power or the clarifying of roles and lines of authority. Consultants might suggest and if desired, provide clergy stress-management or time-management training, or even a vocational assessment so that the clergyperson's talents might be used to the best advantage. Finally, consultants would be available, if requested, to help the various congregational bodies accomplish change in those areas that they saw fit to address.

REOWNING RESPONSIBILITY BY CREATING BOUNDARIES

A boundary is a delineation, something that separates two business entities, two persons, two roles, two geographic areas, two nations, or two concepts. Personal boundaries are recognitions of where one person begins and the other ends. They are composed of awarenesses of what my thoughts, feelings, and sensations are versus what your thoughts, feelings, and sensations are. They are "I" statements. "I" like classical music, and "I" feel disappointed that you do not. And, I do not insist that you also like classical music, although you seem to be unaware that you like Bach. They are statements such as, "I" feel hurt and sad, even if you do not want to believe me.

The development and recognition of personal boundaries is an important part of the growth of the individual as he or she matures and separates from mother, father, and family. It is a constant journey, as we continually discover all the ways we have made assumptions (these are also called projections) about other persons. It is a constant journey, as we continually uncover all the ways that we have swallowed uncritically the thoughts, feelings, and values of our parents and those in authority around us. Now we spit them up and chew on them to see if they really fit who *we* are, this time as individuals. Ethical community requires the pursuit of these awarenesses, in order that we be able to fully respect the thoughts, feelings, values, pain, and personhood of our neighbors. The development of ethical codes, guidelines for intervention in clergy misconduct, psychological screening programs for clerical candidates, and awareness training on the topics of clergy care and sexual abuse and harassment are ways in which religious institutions can begin to create appropriate boundaries to grow themselves into healthier places.[4]

Ethical Codes

As was mentioned earlier, many families of faith do not have formal ethical codes for clergy. Instead, it has been assumed that spiritual leaders would behave ethically, an assumption that has proven to be significantly in error. After all, spiritual leaders, though often regarded as holy, are still very human. Ethical codes provide a yardstick against which to measure the behavior of those who, at their ordination or installation, vow to live by them. It is essential that religious organizations thoughtfully develop, adopt, and publish ethical guidelines for those who minister to their communities. These guidelines must designate sexual misconduct as unethical behavior. In less centralized denominations, it is essential that ethical codes of this sort be adopted by every intermediary judicatory and individual community of faith, so that all are bound by them. It provides only a false sense of security when the national body of a denomination, be it Jewish or Christian, develops guidelines that are not then adopted by the freestanding judicatories and congregations that compose it. We cannot hold clergy or lay ministers to a standard of ethical behavior that has not been described and publicly agreed upon. Furthermore, once these guidelines have been adopted, it is equally important that they be provided in a form that is understandable and visible to the laity *on a continuing basis.*

Guidelines for Intervention in Cases of Alleged Clergy Sexual Misconduct

Specific guidelines for intervention in alleged cases of clergy sexual misconduct, abuse, and harassment, *including operational definitions of these terms,* need also to be thoughtfully developed, adopted, and published by national denominational bodies and then adopted by intermediary judicatories and member congregations. These guidelines need to carefully describe what sexual misconduct is, including a lucid definition of sexual harassment and how misconduct happens. They need to provide a specific, victim-friendly protocol for handling complaints, including the provision of impartial data collectors and advocates for both the victim and the alleged perpetrator. Currently and all to frequently, rather than have any repercussions for the alleged perpetrator, a victim's complaint can mean *the immediate separation of the victim from the community.* This deprives the victim of the needed support for healing that he or she should be able to derive from his or her family of faith. Sexual misconduct, intervention guidelines also need to suggest what is appropriate discipline, and *what is not appropriate discipline.* Decisions in these matters need to be made on a case-to-case basis. It should be reiterated that these descriptions and protocols also need to be presented to the laity in an understandable and visible form on a continuing basis.

Psychological Screening Programs for Candidates

Problems with clergy misconduct can be diminished by screening candidates for ordination prior to their being accepted into the process. Although this is not a procedure without financial encumbrance, its cost is certainly less than that of clergy breakdown and misbehavior. As has been discussed, most clergy come to their vocation with a greater or lesser degree of "baggage" that they have inherited from their families of origin. In addition, the preaching profession attracts persons who have strong narcissistic needs. These individuals not only have a need to be needed, and are therefore in danger of becoming workaholics, but they also often require an idolizing audience. As a result, they frequently are not good team players but instead can become lone rangers and "only" stars. This leaves them vulnerable to erotic entanglements with needy persons who put them on a pedestal. In some cases, candidates may be so dysfunctional as to have a personality disorder. Such persons, although often charismatic, have a tendency to polarize factions within a congregation and in severe cases may be predators.[5]

Psychological screening is useful in the detection of individuals who might be a liability to the religious institution when placed in a leadership role where he or she represents the family of faith. It is also useful in identifying the strengths and weakness of a potential clergyperson, so that the candidate has a greater awareness of his or her own resources, inclinations, and gifts, as well as a sense of the setting in which they might best be used.

Adequate psychological screening involves more than a single interview with a mental health professional. Personality disorders, and in particular persons with narcissistic personality disorder, are difficult to identify. In these cases, an accurate family history and an evaluation of current personal relationships, as well as clinical experience in an ongoing therapeutic relationship, are required in order to make a diagnosis. Psychological testing, however, can get to the heart of the matter more quickly. Accurate testing requires the use of what is called a "full battery'—a series of paper and pencil and projective instruments, along with an intelligence test and a clinical interview, all done by a qualified professional. For data to be considered as representative of the individual, it must reoccur on at least three of the instruments used. Following the administration of the battery, a psychological report describing the instruments used, the results, and the clinical observations made is prepared. Psychological reports must be culturally sensitive, held as highly confidential, and should be fully shared with the candidate. Testing files must also be treated as highly confidential and reviewed only by qualified persons who understand the instruments used, as well as how to read and interpret reports.

Most important, candidates, who have been denied entrance to the ordination process based on the results of psychological testing, should be adequately cared for. This includes compassionate counseling, continuing support, and the discovery of a place or places where their gifts can be utilized as a nonordained person. Individuals who have been gracious enough to offer themselves for ministry, should not be thrown away.

Several denominations currently use this sort of protocol for the screening of their candidates. Some employ the services of independent psychologists, and some utilize vocational counseling centers such as the Center for Career Development and Ministry in Newton Centre, Massachusetts.[6] It has been easier for religious institutions with a more centralized polity to mandate and fund this type of screening. Denominations that do not have top-down power—where individual congregations have considerable autonomy and less financial support from a regional or national body—will have to be more creative, perhaps more courageous, and more fiscally responsible. This is a wise and responsible investment, however, and it can have a large return.

Awareness Training in Clergy Care

Too often, congregations believe that the spiritual leader takes care of the membership, and God takes care of the spiritual leader. This is a great thought, but actually quite idealistic and frankly irresponsible. Clergy and their families have human needs just as everyone else. They, and their families, live under considerable stress—in a fishbowl—and are expected to be symbolic exemplars for the whole community. The compensation clergy receive for the quantity and quality of the work they do is usually meager, at best, when compared to other persons with the same education and years of experience in the field. And the expectations we as congregants have of them is legion. We need to realize that clergy cannot be available twenty-four hours a day, seven days a week. They need ample vacations and a sabbatical, study time, and funds for refreshment courses now and again, if we want stirring sermons. Privacy needs are also important, and congregations might think about developing opportunities for clergy-owned housing. It is hard to get away from the job, relax, and be oneself, when one is living in company-owned housing on the corporate grounds.

We also often expect clergy to be good at all things. Actually, it is rare to find both a good pastor and a good administrator in the same person. This is because good pastors need to be accepting and nonjudgmental, and good administrators need to be good decision makers and not get lost in too many possibilities. Larger, very busy, congregations might think about the possibility of hiring a good pastor and allowing a layperson to do the administrative jobs.

Finally, smaller, less financially well-off congregations might consider hiring a part-time, bivocational spiritual leader instead of compensating a full-time person poorly. Ministerial services could then be augmented by laymembers of the congregation trained for specific tasks, including but not limited to pastoral care, administration, religious education, and even preaching.

Training in Sexual Abuse and Harassment Awareness

In most states, businesses and industries are required by law to provide training for their employees as to what sexual abuse and harassment is, and what to do about it. Some denominations are beginning similar training for clergy. This is certainly useful but not curative until the potential victims, staff and congregants, receive comparable instruction. Most nonclergy, including student ministers, are not aware of denominational sexual misconduct intervention guidelines or reporting protocols even when these important policies have been established. This is because administrative policy, unlike hymnals and prayer books, is rarely published and distributed to the people at large. Clergy, on the other hand, are usually more aware of the workings of the religious body since they have studied the polity and are better hooked into the information pipeline. Guidelines and reporting protocols must be placed in the hands of the laity if these policies and pathways are to adequately do their protective job. Awareness and training as to the nature of sexual abuse and harassment must somehow be incorporated into the life of the congregation if perpetrators are to be held accountable and behavior of this sort is to be diminished.

REOWNING RESPONSIBILITY
THROUGH PROACTIVE CLERGY TRAINING

Proactive clergy training is the responsibility of seminaries, judicatories, congregations, and individual clergy. Spiritual leaders need to be better prepared for the stresses and requirements of ministry. In the past, we have considered the necessary education of clergy to be limited to scriptural knowledge, as well as teaching, liturgical, and pastoral-counseling skills. This is very short-sighted. Not only do clergy need to be educated in the art of administration and such basic things as interviewing and contract negotiation skills, but they need to be educated in ways of supporting themselves spiritually and emotionally. It is a fascinating observation that seminary students are taught how to write prayers but not how to pray! Rarely, if ever, is spiritual direction of the student part of the required seminary curriculum. Somehow, it is assumed that if one manages to get into seminary, one knows how to pray and is not in need of any sharpening of the tools, particularly with regard to the discernment between what is of God and what is of the ego. If only God takes care of the minister, as happens in many cases, the spiritual leader needs to be able to involve him or herself in deep conversation with this resource.

Even beyond this, seminary students rarely spend much time looking at their emotional development or looking at those of their family issues that could contribute to significant problems in ministry. Seminaries may not be able to mandate individual counseling. The cost is significant and could not be part of the academic curriculum since, ethically, such counseling would need to be done outside the formal educational environment and absent of evaluation. Seminaries could, however, mandate a course similar to that taught to training family therapists causes them, in a group format, to examine the issues in their families of origin. This is called "family of origin work" and requires the development of a family map, or genogram, that describes not only the flow of the generations—the names, dates of birth, dates of death, and relationships of one's ancestors and family members—but also various family phenomena. Among these are the reasons for particular deaths, including war, accident, miscarriage, abortion, and suicide; the physical and mental health issues of specific family members, including drug and alcohol addictions and hospitalizations; the dates of marriages, separations, and divorces, along with observed conflictual patterns of interaction; the nature of any family secrets; and an elucidation of family messages. After these awarenesses are developed through the preparation of the genogram, students are then taught to see the repeating patterns of interaction in their families. At this juncture, they may seek their own individual therapy, although they are not required to do so.

In the case of family therapists, this knowledge allows students a degree of preparedness when working with families, so that they do not get entangled in places that are similar to those in their own families of origin. We call this being "stuck." Therapists, clergy-persons, and even consultants can all get stuck when they encounter issues and family messages that are similar to their own and *which they have not worked through.* This is probably what happened to the consultant hired by Hope Church. It is what does happen with clergy who burn out and get in various kinds of trouble. A responsible professional makes developing awarenesses of his or her own issues part of his or her training. When a professional realizes that he or she is stuck because the client or congregation is working with one of the helper's own unfinished issues, the helper—be it therapist, clergyperson, or consultant—goes, at this juncture, for consultation with a supervisor or a professional peer.

When a clergyperson has graduated from seminary without this kind of training as a resource, all is not lost. Denominations at the national and regional level, single congregations, and individual clergypersons can avail themselves of this sort of education from therapists trained in this specialty. Needless to say, it is easier, certainly from a financial perspective, if denominations organize *group* trainings for their clergy. In addition, it has been found from research that clergy-training groups of this sort provide needed support and alleviate some of the sense of loneliness felt by most spiritual leaders.

In one of the studies cited earlier[7] that involved the preparation of a genogram followed by a group, weekend retreat, the participants reported that in addition to increased awareness of family issues and, in particular, the awareness of the presence of family cut-offs, the experience was positive and "door opening" and one that had begun a yet unfinished process. One participant said of the work:

> I walked away from the weekend just realizing how bankrupt my typical approach to life is. . . . I think that the weekend gave me resources to handle that, that was really helpful. . . . I mean the old ways don't work anymore and I have just really needed to be able to say, the whole damn world doesn't depend on me. . . . It's a real groping right now, I don't even understand what I am doing. I mean, it's like learning to walk or something like that."

Another said:

> I think I'm going through a process of cleaning, recleaning who I am, what I want, what I need.

In regard to marital relationship, many of the clergy couples in this study discovered a new willingness to be more open toward each other. They reported:

. . . we kind of began to open up to each other in a different way.

It has made it a good deal easier to talk about things. It certainly has eased some tensions that have existed for a long time.

In spite of all that there seems to be, along with the recognition of these inherited limitations, there seems to be a greater willingness on our part to try to carve out a functional relationship and have a functional family.

It has really given me a fresh outlook. I can see there is real hope.

Finally, the participants reported a sense of group bonding and community support, which was summed up by one member of the group:

. . . it was extremely helpful for us to get up there and see all of it [the genograms] mapped out on the wall, but in a sense the most meaningful part of the whole weekend for me was to kind of bond with that group . . . seeing other people's family histories and seeing that in some sense they are as devastating as ours. . . .

SUMMARY

Personal and corporate existential responsibility reaches beyond the burdens we carry in work, family, and community. Personal responsibility is conscious ownership of one's traits, behaviors, and motivations, coupled with a conscious decision to take an active, rather than a passive role with respect to the environment, be that job, family, or community of faith. Corporate responsibility, or ethical community, is the responsibility of the community toward one another and the environment. A responsible community enables every member to develop to his or her greatest potential in the context of a continuing society. Ethical community chooses an ethic of responsibility instead of a deontological or teleological ethic.

A deontological ethic asks the question, "What is the rule?" and emphasizes an obligation to abstract principles using deductive reasoning. A teleological ethic asks the question, "What is the goal?" and holds the end as ultimately more important than the means. An ethic of responsibility asks, "What is happening?" and then, "What is the fitting response to what is happening?"

Religious institutions that experience broken behavior patterns can begin to reown responsibility by the use of a neutral or independent consultant. This professional must be an impartial observer who begins with a thorough data-collecting process, prepares and delivers a written and oral report of the findings, and suggests ways in which the community of faith might proceed. The consultant must remain in a state of vigilance so as not to be co-opted into abiding by the dysfunctional rules of the system, particularly the rule of secrecy. He or she does not make the community's choices for it but enables the membership to access, strengthen, and use its resources in the mending process. The consultant is a gentle truth-teller who in some cases precipitates a "safe emergency" or a healing crisis, but who can only take a congregation as far as it wants to go on the journey toward wholeness. Consultants are only as effective as they are themselves, whole.

Disclosures of clergy sexual misconduct are experiences of loss, and the task of healing involves progressing through the stages of grief: shock, denial, bargaining, anger, and loss. Once this has occurred, the behavior patterns of the congregation that enabled the problem to evolve need to be addressed.

Preventative maintenance is a second way that religious institutions can reown responsibility. This may be done through early-maintenance consultation, an evaluation of young pastorates that gauges strengths and weaknesses and prescribes corrective measures, as well as enables recognized resources to reach their fullest potential.

Responsibility may also be reowned by the creation of boundaries in the form of carefully developed, adopted, and published ethical codes; operational definitions of sexual misconduct, abuse and harassment which designate these behaviors as unethical; guidelines for intervention in these situations; and screening procedures for prospective candidates for ordination. Awareness training in clergy care and training programs in sexual abuse and harassment also help to create viable boundaries.

Finally, religious institutions can reown responsibility through proactive clergy training in the art of administration, interviewing and contract negotiation, as well as personal spiritual development. In addition, spiritual leaders and their congregations can benefit enormously from clergy, family of origin work, preferably done in a group format with other ministers and rabbis. This work can help clergypersons avoid burnout, become better administrators and counselors, and when done in a group format, can provide needed support and alleviate some of the sense of loneliness felt by most spiritual leaders.

Chapter 11

Postscript:
Becoming a Functional Spiritual Family

In the Judeo-Christian heritage, the tasks of religious communities are five: (1) to provide a place where we can *safely* express and share our experience of faith; (2) to preserve tradition; (3) to create and maintain ethical community; (4) to develop and nurture a sense of mission; and (5) to enable a personal experience of God. In order to do these things, religious communities need healthy communication patterns, adequate resources for dispute resolution, and the recognition that conflict is necessary to growth and change. They also need courage along with the willingness to accept that the path toward spiritual growth is through the shattering of one's illusions. God is mirrored in relationship, and the perfection of relationship is a sacred process.

THE CREATION OF HOLY SPACE

The first task of religious communities is to provide a place for worship and the expression of faith, as well as a safe space for the sharing of the spiritual experiences of the membership. In today's pluralistic society and today's increasingly pluralistic congregations this is no small task indeed. Our theology is frequently the foundation of who we are, and when we rub up against different ideas about God and natural order, we are forced to question our own beliefs. If we do not own our faith structure because we ingested it, uncritically, from our parents and our childhood environment, that sort of questioning can cause a great deal of anxiety, fear, and resultant anger and retribution. Our religious institutions need to en*courage* us in this dialogue by teaching and modeling appropriate communication skills and the ability to learn from difference rather than fight it.

THE PRESERVATION OF TRADITION

Ordinarily, religious institutions are unusually good, even to a fault, at preserving tradition. Tradition includes the spoken word of the prophets, which for Christians includes the teachings of Jesus of Nazareth; the stories of the beginnings of the community; the writings of the faithful as they struggled with their experience of God and their discernment of God's will; the liturgies communities have created to celebrate and re-create that experience; and the history and evolution of the human structure, the institution itself, as it tries, albeit imperfectly, to carry out God's work in the world. Unfortunately, in our tendency to be too concrete, tradition has also tended to include the shape, design, and nature of the worship edifice and the placement of the furniture, and gender bias as well.

THE CREATION AND MAINTENANCE OF ETHICAL COMMUNITY

We have spoken quite a bit about the creation of ethical community. Suffice it to say that in ethical community each member accepts the obligation to be responsible for his or her own actions as well as the welfare of the other. This is a significant task indeed. It requires constant open conversation as a way to discern God's will; personal introspection and an acceptance of self, in order that we might not scapegoat the other; an awareness of power differentials, such that we might not abuse the less advantaged; and a willingness to live with less, to the end that the other might have an equal share, be it material wealth, opportunity, or status. Perhaps most important, the maintenance of ethical community requires its members to assume a great deal of personal responsibility while immersed in a culture that would prefer to point a finger. This is the task of being in the world, while not of the world.

DEVELOPING AND NURTURING A SENSE OF MISSION

A sense of mission provides the cohesive energy that keeps a community together in the face of divisive forces. It is the raison d'etre that reaches beyond ourselves to the world at large. While mission begins at home, with self-nurturance, to be valid it must be transpersonal. For a community to be healthy, mission must extend beyond the boundaries of the family of faith.

Most of us have been brought up to believe that mission has to do with tithing to our religious institution, is a cause we donate money to, or has to do with evangelizing—spreading our religious belief systems to the unbelieving. Of course, mission can be all of these. But, giving money frequently has little to do with the giving of ourselves, and indoctrination is at best disrespectful and at worst destructive when it is imposed upon persons who are otherwise satisfied with their faith systems. Instead, mission in its truest form is the enabling of ethical community in the wider world. It is the demonstration of choice by example. It is the fostering of freedom by the free in spirit who now secure in themselves and their faith, no longer need to enslave their neighbors. It is a different kind of evangelism.

ENABLING AN EXPERIENCE OF GOD

The fourth task of religious communities is to enable an experience of God. These experiences are both private and corporate. Some are ecstatic and can be enabled by good liturgy, while others are the experience of God working in the world through other people. Transcendent experiences, such as Jacob's struggle with the Dark Angel at the river Jabok, or the transfiguration of Jesus of Nazareth witnessed by the disciples on Mt. Tabor, certainly have the power to change, or convert, our life. But it is most important to finally cross the river or go down the mountain again and live out that learning in the community. Then, not only is our life changed, but *lives* are changed and ethical community is created and maintained.

THE CHANGING FACE OF RELIGIOUS INSTITUTIONS

Several prominent writers of our time, including Loren Mead in his book, *The Once and Future Church,*[1] and the Roman Catholic liberation theologians, who have enabled the base community concept to evolve in South America, forecast that the Christian church is in a stage of radical change; the old forms and structures seem to no longer be working very well, and something else is happening. Certainly, there has been a significant drop in the census of all "mainline" Christian denominations, and many North Americans are now unchurched from birth. Likewise, in the Jewish faith, many have ceased attending the temples, schules, and synagogues and remain only secular Jews. In many cases, those who would have been Christians and practicing Jews have sought other ways to express their spirituality by sampling other faiths such as Buddhism, Hinduism, Native American spirituality, gnosticism, and a host of others.

We do not know what the face of religion will look like in the future. Certainly it would seem that the rigidity which tends to be characteristic of mature religious systems, and particularly orthodox religious systems, has in serious ways stifled the creativity that such systems need for renewal. Added to this is the significant betrayal that many persons have suffered at the hands of the members of their own communities, in particular their spiritual leaders. Scapegoating and clergy misconduct are not conducive to a desire to belong, and they seriously hamper all the tasks of families of faith, save the preservation of tradition.

Rigidity, or the difficulty that a system has in changing, adapting, or recreating itself, is proportional to the level of fear experienced by the membership and the main players in the system's hierarchy. We might chalk this fear up to a need for the comfort of the familiar in an uncertain and rapidly changing time. To do so, however, is probably shortchanging ourselves. More than likely, our fear is based on security needs, especially those of religious professionals, as well as our human tendency to not want to gaze squarely at our reflection because we are afraid we will not like what we see.

Rigidity also results when our fear is that we do not have other choices. When we believe that there is only a "right" or a "wrong" instead of side-by-side options, such as a "folk" service at 8:00 a.m., with guitars, and a traditional one at 9:00 a.m. with organ music. Too often we fasten on the notion that fusion—doing and being the same in every way—is the necessary family "glue." Though fusion does tend to make things predictable, it does not equal community. There is more to religious life than wearing a habit.

If our religious institutions are to survive in any form similar to that to which we are accustomed, religious professionals will have to take the major initial responsibility toward shifting priorities from collegial survival to spiritual survival. Clergy, who even in decentralized denominations have for all intents and purposes been the singular guides of our families of faith, will have to give up a quantity of control in the service of shattering the comfortable illusions we have of ourselves. The whole people of God need to see, through impartial lenses, what is broken and what needs to be fixed. And then, devoid of denial, we must proceed with the necessary surgery.

The prophetic vision of the character, Sydney Carton, from Dickens' *Tale of Two Cities* has something very important to say to us about what may be seen as either the unraveling, or the rebirthing, of our religious institutions. Reminding us of the new Jerusalem spoken of by the prophets and by John of Patmos, he says:

> I see . . . long ranks of the new oppressors who have risen on the destruction of the old, perishing by this retributive instrument, before it shall cease out of its present use. I see a beautiful city and a brilliant people rising from this abyss, and, in their struggles to be truly free, in their triumphs and defeats, through many years to come, I see the evil of this time and of the previous time of which this is the natural birth, gradually making expiation for itself and wearing out.

One way or the other, God reminds us that "the new oppressors" shall perish, and something beautiful shall be born. Let us hope that in the process of our transformation from the old Jerusalem to the new Jerusalem, as religious institutions, we will not require too many martyrs. That "in our struggles to be truly free, in [our] triumphs and defeats, through many years to come" we will be able to understand "the evil of this time and of the previous time of which this is the natural birth,"[2] so that gradually we will make expiation for ourselves. Failing that, perhaps we should be comforted that if we, who lead our families of faith, fail to take action, history has noted that God, in his or her wisdom, will.

Appendix

Clinical Presentation of Survivors of Sexual Abuse

Since the human organism is a whole, interrelated entity of body-mind-spirit, it has a variety of ways in which it expresses stress, both psychologically and physically. Because the secrets of incest and clergy misconduct have so many repercussions for the victim, including abandonment, isolation, and becoming a scapegoat, survivors will often deny, repress, or at least minimize their experience, which drives the abuse deeper into the body, causing secondary problems beyond the original emotional anguish. Not uncommonly, the survivor may complain of presenting symptoms such as the following:

- Severe anxiety attacks
- Night terrors
- Depressions
- Mood swings
- Suicidal impulses
- Various (often multiple) phobias
- Compulsions, obsessions
- Eating disorders
- Alcohol or substance abuse
- Conflict avoidance and relationship issues
- Sexual dysfunction such as: diminished sexual desire (all the way to asexuality), impotence, promiscuity, inability to achieve orgasm, need for rape fantasies (S&M, bondage, etc.) to achieve sexual excitement
- Morbid preoccupations such as: fear of choking or dying, self-injury, suicide, committing violent acts
- Miscellaneous cognitive effects including: blocking, auditory or visual hallucinations, feeling like one is in a daze, feeling confused,

Adapted from David Calof, 1988. Conference handout.

difficulty concentrating, difficulty understanding others, going into a trance, feeling one's thoughts are out of control, disorientation, memory disturbance (all the way to amnesia and fugue states), vocalizing words that one did not think to utter, disremembered behaviors
- Miscellaneous somatic complaints including: chronic muscle tension, seizures, palpitations, dizziness, nausea, trembling, gastrointestinal distress, severe headaches, hallucinated body sensations such as choking or assault
- Inexplicable bruises, irritations, or body marks
- Genito-urinary conditions and complaints such as: sexually transmitted diseases, frequent infection, menstrual irregularities, vaginismus, frequent vaginitis, rectal tears, rectal incompetence

Notes

Chapter 1

1. This is not meant to be an exhaustive treatise on family systems theory and the religious institution. For a more in-depth study, please refer to *Generation to Generation: Family Process in Church and Synagogue* by Edwin Friedman (New York: Guilford, 1985) or any of a number of publications by the Alban Institute.

2. Palestine is located in what is known as the Syrophoenician Corridor, the only land route between the trade empires of Egypt, on the Nile Delta, and Babylon, in the Fertile Crescent between the Tigris and Euphrates rivers. As a result, it was economically advantageous for foreign forces to control this area of the Israelite homeland.

3. Under 100 members.

4. In Gen 3:1-5, the Hebrew word used here for "good" is טוֹב , which is variously translated as beautiful, bountiful, enjoyment, feast, fertile, more, pleasant, pleasure, precious, profitable, prosper, rich, etc., and carries more the sense of the "pleasure principle." Correspondingly, the Hebrew word used for "evil," is רַע , which is variously translated as adversity, calamity, misfortune, plight, ruin, unpleasant, vile, etc., and seems to carry more the sense of creaturely discomfort or lack of pleasure. Finally, the Hebrew word for "justice" is מִשְׁפָּט , which in scripture is translated only as just or justice.

5. *The Random House Dictionary of the English Language.* Jess Stern, editor-in-chief and Laurence Urdang, managing editor. New York: Random House, 1973, p. 298.

6. The dynamics of family loyalties are originally the concept of the family therapist Ivan Boszormenyi-Nagy. Boszormenyi-Nagy and Spark (1973) describe loyalty as external expectations coupled with internalized obligations in their book, *Invisible Loyalties: Reciprocity in Intergenerational Family Therapy,* (Reprinted edition) (New York: Brunner/Mazel, 1984).

7. From "Desiderata" in *The Desiderata of Happiness*, by Max Ehrmann (Boulder, CO: Blue Mountain Arts, 1976).

8. This is the precept upon which Martin Luther founded the Reformation. It is noteworthy that in Jewish Conservative congregations, laypersons carefully monitor the reading of the Torah, even while it is read by the rabbi, in order to ascertain that no errors are being made.

Chapter 2

1. This theme has been well elucidated in a book titled, *When Food Is Love: Exploring the Relationship Between Eating and Intimacy,* by Geneen Roth (New York: Plume/Penguin, 1991).

2. A condition characterized by hallucinations, delusions, and paranoia where there is substantial loss of contact with reality, leading to serious impairment in the ability to function in ordinary living situations.

3. Personality disorders result from trauma at a very early age, usually before twenty-four months. As a result, the entire personality development of the individual is interrupted, and in important ways, fixed at early stages of development, leading to substantial perceptual distortion and consequent behavioral dysfunction.

4. Rainer Maria Rilke, *Letters to a Young Poet,* Stephen Mitchell, trans., (New York: Vintage, 1986), pp. 34-35.

5. Gary Dorsey, *Congregation: The Journey Back to Church* (New York: Viking, 1995).

6. William Winslow, "Book Holds Mirror up to Connecticut Church," *United Church News* (July/August, 1995).

7. Publications on sexual abuse and incest did not begin to appear in the literature until the late 1970s and early 1980s.

Chapter 3

1. From my point of view, this is very unfortunate terminology as it tends to reduce persons to *things*.

2. From *The Complete Grimm's Fairy Tales* (New York: Pantheon/Random House, 1944,1972).

3. C. R. Benyei, 1988. "The usefulness of family of origin group work with clergy couples as a tool for professional enhancement and early therapeutic intervention." U. Microfilms.

4. Herbert Anderson, and C. George Fitzgerald, "Use of family systems in preparation for ministry," *Pastoral Psychology* 27(1) (1978), pp. 49-61; Edwin H. Friedman, *Generation to Generation: Family Process in Church and Synagogue* (New York: Guilford, 1985); Candace R. Benyei, *The Usefulness of Family of Origin Group Work with Clergy Couples as a Tool for Professional Enhancement and Early Therapeutic Intervention* (doctoral dissertation) (Ann Arbor, MI: University Microfilms International, 1988).

5. Partially adapted from David Calof, unpublished workshop handout, 1988.

6. There is a wealth of information on this well-researched instrument. See Isabel Briggs Myers, *Gifts Differing*. Palo Alto, CA: Consulting Psychologists Press, Inc., 1980, for a thorough explanation of Jung's typology theory.

7. Roy M. Oswald and Otto Kroeger, *Personality Type and Religious Leadership* (Washington, DC: Alban Institute, 1988), pp. 131-134.

8. For the theoretical basis for this instrument, see Everett L. Shostrom (Ed.), *Actualizing Therapy: Foundations for a Scientific Ethic* (San Diego, CA: Edits Publishers, 1976).

9. Robert R. Knapp, *Handbook for the Personal Orientation Inventory* (San Diego, CA: Edits Publishers, 1976), pp. 48-49.

10. Candace R. Benyei, The Usefulness of Family Origin Work with Clergy Couples.

11. See chapter 9.

Chapter 4

1. Rachel Hosmer, *Gender and God: Love and Desire in Christian Spirituality* (Boston: Cowley, 1986).

2. Erving and Miriam Polster, *Gestalt Therapy Integrated: Contours of Theory and Practice* (New York: Random House, 1973, pp. 99).

3. The family of procreation is the family unit that includes our spouse and our children but not our parents.

4. Harville Hendrix, *Getting the Love You Want: A Guide for Couples* (New York: Harper/Perennial, 1988).

5. David J. Rolfe, "A report on the nurture of clergy families in the Anglican Church of Canada and the Episcopal Church of the United States," a publication of the Office of Pastoral Development of the House of Bishops of the American Episcopal Church (1984).

6. Cited in Richard L. Schuster and Carlynn Reed, *Clergy Family Project* (Report draft) (Bridgeport, CT: Subcommittee on Family of the Social and Specialized Ministry Committee of the Episcopal Church, 1985).

7. Katherine R. Hutchinson, William C. Nichols Jr., and Ira W. Hutchinson, "Therapy for Divorcing Clergy: Implications for Research," *Journal of Divorce* 4(1) (1980), pp. 83-94.

8. Barbara B. Zigmund, Adair T. Lummis, and P. M. Y. Chang, *Second Preliminary Report of the Ordained Men and Women Study* (Hartford, CT: Hartford Seminary Center for Social and Religious Research, 1995).

9. Lucille Lavender, *They Cry Too* (New York: Hawthorn, 1976); Mary L. Bouma, *Divorce in the Parsonage* (Minneapolis, MN: Bethany Publishing, 1979); Donna Sinclair, *The Pastor's Wife Today* (Nashville, TN: Abingdon, 1981); Earl K. Ziegler, *Divorce Among the Church of the Brethern Clergy: Role Expectations as Contributory Factors* (unpublished doctoral dissertation) (Lancaster, PA: Lancaster Theological Seminary, 1981); Sarah R. Brown, "Clergy Divorce and Remarriage," *Pastoral Psychology* 30(3) (1982), pp. 187-197; Richard A. Goodling and Cheryl Smith, "Clergy Divorce: A Survey of Issues and Emerging Ecclesiastical Structures," *Journal of Pastoral Care* 37(4), (1983), pp. 277-291; Edwin Friedman, *Generation to Generation: Family Process in Church and Synagogue* (New York: Guilford, 1985).

10. Dag Hammarskjöld, *Markings*. Translated from the Swedish by Leif Sjöberg and W. H. Auden. (New York: Alfred A. Knopf, 1965, p. 85.)

11. According to *The Diagnostic and Statistical Manual of Mental Disorders,* Fourth Edition (Washington, DC: American Psychiatric Association, 1994).

12. See Mircea Eliade's works, *Shamanism: Archaic Techniques of Esctasy* (Princeton, NJ: Princeton/Bollingen, 1972) and *Rites and Symbols of Initiation: The Mysteries of Birth and Rebirth* (New York: Harper and Row, 1958).

13. See Henri J. M. Nouwen's work, *The Wounded Healer* (Garden City, NY: Image/Doubleday, 1972).

Chapter 5

1. This definition is adapted from the policy of sexual misconduct by the Iowa Conference of the United Church of Christ (UCC) and is based on federal law regarding sexual harassment. In 1980, the Equal Opportunity Commission (EEOC) expanded the definition of sexual harassment to include any unwanted verbal and nonverbal sexual behavior. The EEOC ruled that: *sexual harassment, like racial harassment, generates a harmful atmosphere . . . . employees should be afforded a working environment free of discriminatory intimidation whether based on sex, race, religion, or national origin* ("Rules and Regulations," p. 25024).

2. Adapted from UCC Iowa Conference policy and the Fifth Draft of the UCC manual on Pastoral Misconduct.

3. From *The Charge of the Light Brigade*, by Alfred Lord Tennyson.

4. According to *The Diagnostic and Statistical Manual of Mental Disorders,* Fourth Edition (Washington, DC: American Psychiatric Association, 1994).

5. Ibid.

6. Sexual masochism can also be dangerous, but only to the individual with the disorder.

7. Personal correspondence with Marvin A. Steinberg, PhD, 1996.

8. Marvin A. Steinberg, "Sexual Addiction and Compulsive Gambling," *American Journal Preventive Psychiatry and Neurology, 2*(3) (May 1990).

9. See Chapter 4.

10. This is the title of a very wonderful book by the well-known psychotherapist, Irvin Yalom, MD, that explains transference love quite well, and in an anecdotal form. *Love's Executioner and Other Tales of Psychotherapy* (New York: Basic Books, 1989).

Chapter 6

1. A. W. Richard Sipe, *Sex, Priests, and Power: Anatomy of a Crisis* (New York: Brunner/Mazel, 1995), p. 119.

2. See the excellent case study and analysis presented by Marie M. Fortune in her book, *Is Nothing Sacred?: The Story of a Pastor, the Women He Sexually Abused, and the Congregation He Nearly Destroyed* (San Francisco, CA: HarperSanFrancisco, 1989).

3. In the Middle East, a married woman, who has been found to have had intercourse with a partner outside the marriage, is condemned to death by religious law. In

some Asian cultures, a married woman, who has been found to have had sexual relations outside the marriage, faces certain divorce.

4. Sipe (1995) reports that a high percentage of Roman seminarians are primary victims of sexual abuse received at the hands of seminary staff and superiors.

5. Again, see the account in Marie Fortune's book, *Is Nothing Sacred?*

6. The Reverend Margo Maris, cochair of the Sexual Exploitation Committee of the General Convention of the American Episcopal Church, notes that barely 1 percent of charges of sexual misconduct are proven false. (The Episcopal News Service, February 8, 1996, p. 5).

7. The American Episcopal Church, at its 1994 General Convention, enacted a substantial change in its canon law with respect to ecclesiastical discipline, especially with respect to clergy sexual misconduct. Among the changes were more flexibility for victims in filing charges and input in sentencing offenders, and added due process for clergy, including the removal of bishop prosecutors and barring chancellors from having a role in presentments or trials. Clergy are also barred from appealing ecclesiastical sentences in secular courts.

Chapter 7

1. *Tanakh—the Holy Scriptures: The New JPS Translation According to the Traditional Hebrew Text* (New York: Jewish Publication Society, 1988).

2. Louis Ginzberg, *The Legends of the Jews 5* (Philadelphia: Jewish Publication Society, 1968 p. 171).

3. This might serve as a corrective to the unfortunately common Christian notion that the Jewish God, the God of the Hebrew scriptures, is a vengeful God. God is always merciful, and we would do well to mirror this image in all circumstances.

4. This is true only for the so-called mainline religious institutions and does not include devil worship and several other groups that sacrifice chickens or other small animals.

5. Excellent descriptions of this problem, along with some of the remedies, may be found in "Afterpastors in Troubled Congregations," by Darline K. Haskin and "Further Issues for Afterpastors," by Nancy Myer Hopkins in Nancy M. Hopkins and Mark Laaser, eds., *Restoring the Soul of a Church: Healing Congregations Wounded by Clergy Sexual Misconduct* (Washington, DC: Alban Institute, 1995).

6. See the articles in *Restoring the Soul of a Church, Part II: Secondary Victims.*

7. Darline K. Haskin, "Afterpastors in Troubled Congregations," in *Restoring the Soul of a Church: Healing Congregations Wounded by Clergy Sexual Misconduct.*

8. Charles Dickens, *A Tale of Two Cities* (New York: Penguin, 1988), pp. 403-404.

Chapter 8

1. The Greco-Roman culture was partriarchal and repressive of women, who were treated suspiciously and were functionally without rights.
2. David Gelman and Debra Rosenburg, "Family Secrets," *Newsweek Magazine* (February 24, 1997), p. 30.
3. Ibid.
4. Ibid., p. 27.
5. A nice elucidation of this is given in "The Unhealed Wounders," by Richard Irons and Katherine Roberts in Nancy M. Hopkins and Marl Laaser, eds. *Restoring the Soul of a Church: Healing Congregations Wounded by Clergy Sexual Misconduct* (Washington, DC: Alban Institute, 1995).

Chapter 9

1. See C. Jeff Woods book, *Congregational Megatrends* (Washington, DC: Alban Institute, 1996).
2. In this denomination, the committee on ministry is responsible for the examination of candidates for their fitness for ministry and for ratifying ecclesiastical standing, as well as judgment and discipline in ethical matters.
3. It is generally not advisable for junior clergy to remain in place after the calling of a new senior pastor, since loyalty issues and personality clashes can interfere with the establishment of the senior pastor's leadership role. In some denominations, such as the American Episcopal Church, it is standard and recognized protocol to remove the junior associate when a new senior minister is installed.
4. From Shakespeare's work, *Macbeth*.
5. Chelton Knudson in *Restoring the Soul of a Church: Healing Congregations Wounded by Clergy Sexual Misconduct*, Nancy Myer Hopkins and Mark Laaser (Eds.), (Washington, DC: Alban Institute, 1995).

Chapter 10

1. This concept was first developed by H. Richard Niebuhr in *The Responsible Self* (New York: Harper and Row, 1963).
2. See the publication list of the Alban Institute, Suite 433 North, 4550 Montgomery Avenue, Bethesda, MD, 20814-3341, (800) 486-1318, ext. 244 or that of the Mennonite Conciliation Service, 21 South Street, P.O. Box 500, Akron, PA 17501-0500, (717) 859-3889.
3. The various writings of Elizabeth Kübler-Ross are useful here.
4. The American Episcopal Church, as was noted earlier, responded in 1994 by changing its canon law with regards to disciplinary procedures in cases of sexual misconduct. According to a personal communication with the Reverend Canon Richard Tombaugh, of the Diocese of Connecticut, all dioceses are now

required to do background checks on clergy, whether or not they are in the process of changing employment. Some dioceses are more thorough than others, as the process is not uniform. The New England region currently requires questionnaires to be filled out by all of an individual's former employers and educational institutions, within the past fifteen years. The information is collated and kept on file nationally by an independent archival records research firm. The Presbyterian Church (USA) responded in 1993 with its *Sexual Misconduct Policy* and its *Procedures* legislation that address disciplinary procedures. It has recently drafted a model misconduct policy to guide the process for individual Presbyteries. However, according to a 1997 personal correspondence with Zane K. Buxton of the Office of the General Assembly, presbytery leaders and individuals who work with the leaders in the call referral system have been reluctant to put into force a certification *by the Presbytery* of the accuracy of the material, with respect to involvement in sexual misconduct, as indicated (or not indicated) by clergypersons on their personal information forms. Therefore, background checks are currently left up to the calling body. The national denominational headquarters of the United Church of Christ responded in 1994 by creating the *Fifth Draft on Pastoral Misconduct*. According to a 1997 personal communication with the Reverend Gene Kraus of the UCC National Office of Church Life and Leadership, new clergy, or clergy who are changing jobs, must have on file at the National Office a profile that includes a background check and consent for information verification. As in the Presbyterian Church, this information form is filled out by the clergyperson. Also similar to the Presbyterian Church, the calling body is ultimately responsible for determining whether or not the information provided by the clergyperson is accurate. Reverend Kraus did add, however, that whenever conference ministers or other judicatory officials become aware of, *and report to the National Office*, negative information with regard to any sort of misconduct or legal proceedings, profiles are pulled and amended.

5. See Chapter 4.

6. The Center for Career Development and Ministry, 70 Chase Street, Newton Centre, MA 02159-2233, (617) 969-7750.

7. Candace R. Benyei, *The Usefulness of Family of Origin Group Work with clergy Couples as a Tool for Professional Enhancement and Early Therapeutic Intervention* (doctoral dissertation) (Ann Arbor, MI: University Microfilms International, 1988).

8. "Cut-offs" are instances where family members have relocated themselves, usually to a geographically distant place, and have ceased communicating with one another for extended periods of time.

Chapter 11

1. Loren B. Mead, *The Once and Future Church: Reinventing the Congregation for a New Mission Frontier* (Washington, DC: Alban Institute, 1991).

2. Charles Dickens, *A Tale of Two Cities* (New York: Penguin Books, 1859/1988), p. 404.

Glossary

afterpastor: A clergyperson who follows the tenure of a colleague who engaged in sexual misconduct.

a "good enough" holding environment: An environment in which an infant feels sufficiently supported, both physically and emotionally, such that normal development is enabled.

archetype: Symbolic manifestations of the inner world of ideas, images, and dreams, that have universal meaning.

bad object: An internalized image that contains all the frustrating, frightening, and depriving impressions of the primary caretakers.

centralized, or episcopal, polity: A polity in which the decision-making power flows from the top of the hierarchy down to the congregational level.

committed relationship: A relationship in which one covenants not to abandon the other in stressful circumstances.

countertransference: The phenomenon wherein the counselor transfers his or her good/bad objects, issues, or emotions on to the client and imagines them to be aspects of the client rather than of the self of the counselor.

covenant: The conscious, willful acceptance of an obligation to another party.

deflection: The redirecting of energy from the source of irritation to a safer object, cause, or activity.

denial: The process of convincing oneself that what is happening is not really happening.

deontological ethic: An ethic that bases judgment upon certain abstract laws or principles.

differentiation: The process of discovering oneself as different, unique, individual, and separate from the environment, while at the same time having the ability to stay connected to it.

early-childhood decision: A behavioral, survival decision made in early childhood, that has passed out of adult consciousness.

emotional withdrawal: The withholding of emotional support, comfort, and nurturance from another. An extreme form of this is the practice of "shunning."

emotionally empty: The condition of unrequited longing and lack of emotional resources, resulting from a childhood deprived of emotional nurturance and support.

ethic of responsibility: An ethic that strives to make a fitting response to persons in the context of their situations and implies accountability in the context of continuing community.

family loyalty: The obligation to obey the family rules and elevate the perceived needs of the family over that of the individual.

family of faith: The religious community of which an individual is a part.

family of origin: The immediate and extended family in which one grew up.

family of procreation: The marital pair and any children.

family projection system: A term coined by the family therapist, Murray Bowen, to indicate the way in which family members project an issue or an inner representation of themselves onto family members (often a child), who then frequently tend to live out the role or the issue as if it were themselves.

family rules: Formal, informal, or tacit agreements that bind family members to behave in certain ways. Formal rules are conscious, "published," and subject to amendment, such as a 10 p.m. curfew. Informal rules are consciously but silently agreed upon and are difficult to change since they are not discussed. Tacit rules are unconscious and are usually communicated nonverbally, by modeling.

"free" church or congregational polity: A polity in which the decision-making power rests at the congregational level, rather than at the judicatory or national denominational level.

genogram: A family map of relationships that includes dates of births, deaths, suicides, abortions or miscarriages, marriages, separations, and divorces, as well as information about significant physical and mental health issues, substance abuse, ethnicity, gender preference, education, occupation, and environmental stressors.

good object: An internalized image containing all the nurturing, satisfying and comforting impressions of the primary caretakers.

hearsay: Data that was not collected from firsthand experience but was obtained from the observations of another.

highly defended: The condition, arising out of unconscious self-criticism, of needing to be unaware of one's pain or the impact of one's behavior upon another.

incest: Sexual activity between persons, other than the marital pair, who are closely related by blood or marriage.

interpersonal boundary: The awareness of what one's emotions, thoughts, issues, and desires are apart from those of another.

learned incompetence: The sense, gained from verbal and nonverb al family messages, that one is incapable of decision making or performance.

minimization: Diminishing the importance of reality.

neutral: An impartial observer who has the capacity to stay aware of his or her own biases and not let them prejudice the outcome of a conversation or negotiation.

object relations: A school of psychodynamic theory, heavily influenced by Margaret Mahler, that posits the creation of internal images of the primary caretakers, or "objects," by the infant. It also includes the dynamics of the ensuing relationship between the infant, the caretakers, and the internal representations.

"old business": Unresolved, emotional conflicts usually from one's family of origin.

overidentify: To lose the boundary between oneself and the other and become the other's pain, shame, or anxiety.

parentified: The condition in which the family hierarchy is reversed, and children develop the expectation that they are to care for the adults, instead of the other way around.

pedophile: A developmentally arrested individual, usually with poor impulse control, who has difficulty with age appropriate, emotionally intimate, relationships and is sexually attracted to children.

personality disorder: A pervasive, developmental, psychological dysfunction, rooted in early-childhood trauma, that causes particular maladaptive patterns of behavior unsuitable to adult operations.

predator: An individual who derives a sense of power, status, and well-being through the sexual abuse of other persons.

projection: The process of playing the image of an emotion, or of an inner self-representation (much like projecting a movie picture), onto another person and imagining that the picture is them, instead of part of oneself. For instance, I might project *my* anger onto another and imagine that *they* are angry, not me.

projective identification: The tendency to make assumptions about a person based on our prior experience with one or more of our powerful caretakers, whom the individual in some way resembles.

pseudoactualized: The condition of having a cognitive awareness of desired values without emotional/behavioral manifestation.

psychosis: The inability to distinguish the here-and-now from the imaginary world including, but not limited to, a loss of a sense of self.

rationalization: The process of convincing oneself of the goodness of something harmful.

repression: The forceful forgetting of experience.

scapegoat: An individual who is chosen to bear the blame for another's misdeeds.

secondary victim of sexual abuse: persons who have not been the immediate recipients of unwanted sexual attention but who, nonetheless, suffer peripheral consequences of the abuse.

sexual addict: An individual with a compulsive sexual behavior or obsessive emotional attachment to sexual fantasies, which have a pervasive negative impact on the person's life.

shamanic call: A vocation traditionally associated with witchdoctors and aboriginal medicine persons, which is initiated by a spontaneous character-restructuring or conversion, usually perceived by the community as an illness. As the individual learns to heal him or herself, he or she develops the tools for the healing of others.

situational abuser: An individual who does not habitually abuse but who may abuse when placed in stressful situations—when his or her emotional needs are not being met.

splitting: A phenomenon observed in persons who have not integrated their good and bad objects as a part of normal development. The internalized images are projected outward upon another, who is alternately seen as all good or all bad.

symbolic exemplar: A phrase coined by Rabbi Jack Bloom. A person who is assumed, or obligated to be, a paragon of right behavior.

symbolic incest: The emotional marriage of a parent and child, in which the child is elevated to the parental level of the hierarchy and expected to partner the parent.

teleological ethic: An ethic that justifies the means in the service of a desired end.

transference: A special case of projection in which the good or bad aspects of the primary caretakers, or internalized objects, are transferred onto another through the use of the unconscious imagination.

transference love: The transference of one's good object or dispossessed positive aspects onto another, along with the desire to be joined with this satisfying, unacknowledged portion of the self. This phenomenon is usually accompanied by powerful feelings of self-acceptance, longing, and sexual arousal.

triangle: An anxious relationship between two persons who perceive themselves as having unequal power and who use a third individual (often a child, a peer, or a sibling) to communicate indirectly, in order to attenuate the anxiety.

unresolved grief: Depression, melancholia, and dysfunctional behavior problems associated with an incomplete grieving process and acceptance of loss.

vocation: An employment that involves one's passion and gives meaning to life.

wounded healer: A person who, through the healing of his or her own psychological wounds, discovers the tools to enable the healing of others.

Index

Abandonment, emotional, power
    of, 64,110,111
Abandonment anxiety, human, 9
Abuse
    clerical, 53
    rage and anger, 107
Accountability, 146
Adolescents, resistance stage, 76
"Adult children," 76-77
Adultery
    ethics of, 148
    punishment in ancient Israel, 105
Advantage, relationship determinant,
    7
"Afterpastors," 93-94,154
American Association of Marriage
    and Family Therapists,
    suspension of members,
    70-71
American Episcopal Church
    clerical divorce rate, 49,50
    false accusations, 81
Amish, discipline of, 8
Anger
    discharge of, 107
    families of origin, 26-28
    grieving stage, 152,153
    Hope Church, 140
    religious institutions and, 121-122
    role in scapegoating, 90
Animal force, 64,65
Animal sacrifice, mainline
    communities
    of faith, 86
Antisocial personality disorder
    clergy with, 54-55
    sexual predator, 69
Apollo, Greek god, 102

Archetypes, 40
Assumptions, family projection
    system, 8
Authority
    Hope Church, 138
    power of, 64-65
Awareness training, clerical,
    156-157,160
Azazel, tale of, 85-86

Bad object, object relations theory,
    34
Bargaining, grieving stage, 152-153
Behavior patterns, broken, mending
    of, 153
Birth order, scapegoating and, 88-89
Blaming the victim, Hope Church,
    140
Boundaries, creating, 145,156-161
Boundary, drawing a, 76
Bowen, Murray, family therapist, 2
"Brain washing," 114,115
Bride of Christ, Christian metaphor,
    14
Briggs, Katharine Cook, 39
Burnout, clerical, 53

Calling, 49,50,51
Caretaker
    child's view of, 34
    control over, 33
Center for Career Development
    and Ministry, 159
Character disorders, development of,
    54
Childish behavior, family
    proscription on, 38,39

Order Your Own Copy of
This Important Book for Your Personal Library!

UNDERSTANDING CLERGY MISCONDUCT IN RELIGIOUS SYSTEMS
Scapegoating, Family Secrets, and the Abuse of Power

_____ in hardbound at $29.95 (ISBN: 0-7890-0451-8)

_____ in softbound at $19.95 (ISBN: 0-7890-0452-6)

COST OF BOOKS_____

OUTSIDE USA/CANADA/
MEXICO: ADD 20%_____

POSTAGE & HANDLING_____
(US: $3.00 for first book & $1.25
for each additional book)
Outside US: $4.75 for first book
& $1.75 for each additional book)

SUBTOTAL_____

IN CANADA: ADD 7% GST_____

STATE TAX_____
(NY, OH & MN residents, please
add appropriate local sales tax)

FINAL TOTAL_____
(If paying in Canadian funds,
convert using the current
exchange rate. UNESCO
coupons welcome.)

☐ **BILL ME LATER:** ($5 service charge will be added)
(Bill-me option is good on US/Canada/Mexico orders only;
not good to jobbers, wholesalers, or subscription agencies.)

☐ Check here if billing address is different from
shipping address and attach purchase order and
billing address information.

Signature_____

☐ **PAYMENT ENCLOSED: $**_____

☐ **PLEASE CHARGE TO MY CREDIT CARD.**

☐ Visa   ☐ MasterCard   ☐ AmEx   ☐ Discover
☐ Diners Club
Account #_____

Exp. Date_____

Signature_____

Prices in US dollars and subject to change without notice.

NAME_____

INSTITUTION_____

ADDRESS_____

CITY_____

STATE/ZIP_____

COUNTRY_____ COUNTY (NY residents only)_____

TEL_____ FAX_____

E-MAIL_____
May we use your e-mail address for confirmations and other types of information? ☐ Yes   ☐ No

Order From Your Local Bookstore or Directly From
The Haworth Press, Inc.
10 Alice Street, Binghamton, New York 13904-1580 • USA
TELEPHONE: 1-800-HAWORTH (1-800-429-6784) / Outside US/Canada: (607) 722-5857
FAX: 1-800-895-0582 / Outside US/Canada: (607) 772-6362
E-mail: getinfo@haworth.com
PLEASE PHOTOCOPY THIS FORM FOR YOUR PERSONAL USE.

BOF96